Writing

A Survival Guide

Joyce Kupsh
and
Rhonda Rhodes

Copyright © 2022 Joyce Kupsh and Rhonda Rhodes.

All rights reserved. No part of this book may be reproduced, stored, or transmitted by any means—whether auditory, graphic, mechanical, or electronic—without written permission of both publisher and author, except in the case of brief excerpts used in critical articles and reviews. Unauthorized reproduction of any part of this work is illegal and is punishable by law.

ISBN: 979-8-88640-289-6 (sc)
ISBN: 979-8-88640-290-2 (hc)
ISBN: 979-8-88640-291-9 (e)

Because of the dynamic nature of the Internet, any web addresses or links contained in this book may have changed since publication and may no longer be valid. The views expressed in this work are solely those of the author and do not necessarily reflect the views of the publisher, and the publisher hereby disclaims any responsibility for them.

One Galleria Blvd., Suite 1900, Metairie, LA 70001
1-888-421-2397

Acknowledgement

A special thank you goes to Joe Cruz.

Joyce Kupsh - jkupsh@cox.net
Rhonda Rhodes - drrhondarr@gmail.com

Contents

Introduction x

Chapter 1—Organizing 1
   Purposes 2
      Inform 2
      Interpret 3
      Recommend 3
      Persuade 3
   Types of Writing 4
      Essay 4
      Research Report 4
      Resume 5
      Cover Letter 6
      Case Study Analysis 6
      Case Study 7
      Feasibility Study 7
      Strategic Plan 8
      Business Plan 8
      Business Proposal 9
      Evaluation Report 9
      Synthesis Report 9
      Assessment/Audit Report 10
      Technical Report 10
      Follow-up Report 10
      Press Release 10
      Miscellaneous 10
   Format Styles 10
      E-mail, Memo, Letter 11
      Form 12
      Report 12
      Newsletter 12
      Brochure 13
      Magazine, Booklet, or Manual 14
      Social Media 15

Blogs 17
    Reasons to Blog 18
    Starting a Blog 18
Parts of a Report 19
    Executive Summary/Abstract 20
    Contents 21
    Introduction 21
    Body 22
    Appendices 22
    Bibliography/References/Resources 22

Chapter 2—Starting 25
Planning 26
    Purposes or Objectives 26
    Target Audience 27
    Time Schedule 27
    Overall Plan 28
Researching 29
    Secondary Data 29
    Primary Data 29
Outlining 30
    Preparation 30
    Evaluation 31

Chapter 3—Referencing 33
Plagiarism 34
    Common Forms of Plagiarism 34
    Avoiding Plagiarism 35
Citing Sources 36
    Quoting 37
    Paraphrasing 39
    Summarizing 39
Technology-Based Tools 40
    Reference Management Software 41
    Reference Checkers 41
    Citation Creators 41
    Word Processing Software 41

- Citing Sources 42
  - Parenthetical 42
  - Endnotes 43
  - Footnotes 43
- Using Style Manuals 43

Chapter 4—Writing 47
- Objectivity 48
  - Informal 48
  - Formal 48
- Conciseness 49
  - Irrelevant Information 50
  - Redundancy 50
  - Clutter and Clichés 50
  - Extra Phrases 51
  - Implied Ideas 52
  - Abstract or General Words 52
- Coherence 53
  - Repetition 53
  - Transition 53
- Tone 55
  - Positive versus Negative 55
  - Active versus Passive 56
  - Expletives 56
  - Pronouns 56
  - Bias-Free Language 57
- Emphasis 58
- Variety 58
- Comprehensive 59

Chapter 5—Polishing 61
- Abbreviations 62
- Acronyms 62
- Capitalization 63
- Italics 65
- Numbers 66
- Punctuation 67
  - Apostrophe 67

    Colon 68
    Comma 68
    Dash 69
    Diagonal 69
    Ellipsis 69
    Exclamation Point 69
    Hyphen 69
    Parentheses 70
    Period 70
    Question Mark 70
    Quotation Marks 71
    Semicolon 71
Spelling 72
Word Division 73

Chapter 6—Producing 77
Fonts 77
    Classifications 78
    Variations 80
    Sizes 81
    Line Spacing 81
    Alignment 82
Color 83
Paper 83
    Type 84
    Weight 84
    Size 84
Layout 85
    Page Orientation 85
    Margins 85
    Column Size 85
    Blank Space 86
    Headings and Subheadings 86
    Page Numbers 87
    Headers and Footers 87
    Binding 88
    Cover 88
Graphics 88

Chapter 7—Finishing ... 93
Editing ... 94
- Substance ... 94
- Style ... 94
- Consistency ... 94

Proofreading ... 95
- Techniques ... 95
- Tips ... 96

Bonus Section ... 99

Designing and Delivering Presentations ... 99
Designing Slides ... 103
- Template Choice ... 105
- Two Parts—Title & Body ... 105
- Color ... 107
- Font Choice ... 109
- Big Is Better ... 111
- Less Is Better ... 113
- Graphics ... 117
- Music/Sounds/Videos ... 119
- Animations ... 121
- Transitions ... 123
- Speaker Notes ... 125

Delivering Presentations ... 127
- Practice/Rehearse/Timing ... 129
- Equipment Setup ... 131
- Speaker Position ... 133
- Speaking Essentials ... 135

Checklists ... 139

Index ... 161

Introduction

> ***Today,*** *our communications have many formats. You text all the time to your BFFs. OMG you LOL and give TMI. You tweet with Twitter and post on Facebook and Instagram. BTW, you blog, email, chat, and IM.*
>
> —Rhodes and Kupsh

Many methods of communicating are used in the twenty-first century. Telephones, letters, reports, and faxes are still used; but now we also use things such as blogging, texting, instant messaging, e-mail, voice mail, Facebook, and Twitter. These new methods have a language entirely different from the established communication language of the working world.

However, to succeed in college, on the job, and in life, you must be able to produce top-notch written communications. Effective writing is planned, researched, and outlined; and in some cases, referencing is required. Different formats for special purposes and audiences can help to make your writing more attractive. Written communications can be one page or numerous pages. But all writing should include correct grammar, punctuation, and spelling, as well as objectivity, conciseness, thoroughness, coherence, and an eye catching format. You must be aware of the types, format choices, and the parts of written communications.

INTRODUCTION

Writing—A Survival Guide will help you with the essentials of producing effective written communications. Whether you are writing a blog, essay, resume, a case study, a research report, or a strategic plan; the Checklists at the end of the book will help ensure your written communication is successful for its intended purpose. The material appears in an orderly arrangement. However, you may choose to refer to a particular section as needed.

CHAPTER 1

Organizing

> ***Organize, organize, organize!*** *Organization is absolutely critical to a successful communication. Before you write a word, you should spend time thinking and arranging. You must consider the purpose, type, format, style, and parts of your written work.*
>
> —Rhodes and Kupsh

Organizing means to arrange or order things so that they can be found or used easily and quickly, according to the dictionary.

The time you spend thinking and arranging—organizing—will pay off throughout the completion of your writing. When organizing your written communication, you need to think about the following:

- Purpose of the writing
- Type of writing that works best
- Format that will be the most effective.

Purposes

Written communication must have a reason. The reason may be to inform, interpret, recommend, persuade, or some combination of these reasons.

Inform

Written communications that inform may tell the status or progress of a situation. Blogs and social media are popular means of informing in today's technological world. Examples of social media are Facebook, which informs friends of our status, LinkedIn, which is used by people in the business world, or Twitter, which shares an opinion in 144 characters or less. Even though the various types of social media inform, they require special care in their organization and writing.

Examples of various types of communications that inform are as follows:

- *Blogs*—provide information on every topic imaginable.
- *Resume*—provides information about a person, as well as skills, education, experience, and references.
- *Essay*—expresses and relates different thoughts on topics.
- *Company annual report*—tells the shareholders the status of the company.
- *Sales report*—provides the sales performance for a week/ month/ year.
- *Construction report*—updates the progress a company has made toward completion of the new company headquarters.
- *Procedures*—includes procedures to be followed.
- *Documentation*—describes occurrences or events.
- *Financial reports*—includes such things as income and expense statement, balance sheet, credit standing showing financial position
- *Social media*—informs colleagues of your status.

Interpret

Rather than simply stating the condition, interpretive writing advances to a higher level, going beyond the facts and including an analysis or interpretation of the facts. Examples of this type of writing are:

- *Sales or marketing*—analyzes the reasons for an increase or decrease in a given period of time.
- *Research and development*—describes the performance standards of a new product.
- *Scientific or technical*—investigates numerous activities.
- *Financial*—explains the budget needs for a new venture.

Recommend

- Writing may include information and provide an interpretive analysis and then go to the next step of providing solutions or recommendations. Any of the examples listed under the previous category may include a recommendation. Other examples are:

- *Case studies, business proposals, and many other types*—includes facts and ends with recommendations.
- *Theses or dissertations*—investigates a topic by conducting original research—such as a survey, a series of interviews, an experimental study—and analyzes the results, and providing recommendations for the future.
- *Investigation and analysis of a product or company*—including one or more recommendations of how improvements can be made.

Persuade

An attempt to persuade or generate action of some type could be the purpose of writing. A persuasive communication might contain elements of all three previous types—inform, interpret, and recommend—but then goes one more step and adds an emotional appeal to the recommendation. Examples are as follows:

- *Essay*—expressing a desire with reasons for being admitted to a college/university
- *Sales proposals*—soliciting new business from clients.
- *Requests*—suggesting a change of some type
- *Solicitation of funds*—requesting funds for a given task or activity
- *Cover letters*—persuading a prospective employer to grant an interview or explain a report being sent.

Types of Writing

Many types of writing are required today. Yet, in general, written communication has commonalities and similar requirements. The information provided in this book applies to any type of writing. However, your writing may fall into one of the following types.

Essay

An essay is a short paper on an assigned topic. The purpose of such an assignment may be to check your knowledge and opinion, as well as creativeness and writing skills. Teachers in elementary and high schools may ask for essays in an exam. Colleges/universities frequently require essays as an entrance selection process or as examinations once enrolled in classes. Writing an opinion article to a newspaper or magazine is another use of an essay.

Essay
Purpose and/or problem statement
Introduction
Body—a paragraph for each point or topic
Conclusion

Research Report

A research report is routinely assigned in schools and universities. This type of report addresses a particular problem or topic and can include material found in existing scholarly journals, magazines, newspapers, books, websites, as well as original research.

Research Report
Introduction and topic, issue, or problem statement
Review of relevant existing sources
Original data
Findings
Summary, conclusions, and recommendations
Bibliography, references, and resources

Resume

Most of the population will at some time need to write a resume and cover letter. A resume may result in getting an interview for the job leading to a career. The format of the resume depends upon many factors. Some companies may want a one-page resume while others may desire more details. In general, a resume may contain sections such as objectives, professional profile, qualifications, skills, and references.

When you want to develop your resume, do a web search for resumes. Many sites are available that help to build a resume for an individual's special needs. The sites will provide choices such as classic, executive, professional, deluxe, contemporary, emphasis, chronological (or reverse chronological), artistic, charismatic, and many more. Some of the websites offer samples by the type of industry for where you are applying. For example, resumes for an office worker, a teacher, a nurse, a housekeeper, and marketing/sales would require different information and a unique slant.

Resume
Personal information—name, address, email, phone number
Work experience—name of the company, address, phone, dates employed, supervisor

Education—all schools attended, degrees, dates of attendance, areas of emphasis
Expertise—specific areas where you excel
References—names and phone numbers of people who will speak positively about you

Cover Letter

Cover letters or e-mails are frequently needed when sending another document such as a resume. Many applications for employment request a cover letter/e-mail to accompany the resume. An effective cover letter being sent with a resume should briefly summarize why you would be good for a specific job. Many cover letters include the following.

Cover Letter/E-mail
State the specific position for which you are applying
Summarize your qualifications and how they fit the job
Request an interview

Case Study Analysis

Numerous college classes use case study analysis as part of the learning process. An effective case study analysis can vary but usually includes the following components.

Case Study Analysis
Investigate and analyze the company's history and growth.
SWOT—strengths, weaknesses, opportunities, threats
Analysis of the competition and the whole external environment
Corporate-level strategy and issues
Business-level strategy and issues
Identify possible strategic actions
Recommend actions supported by the findings
Bibliography, references, and resources

Case Study

A case study allows you to present a product, service, or solution to a prospective client. A case study should be written with a specific goal or client in mind.

Case Study
Company profile
Business situation
Technical situation
Issues of importance
Proposed solution
Benefits
Products and services
Recommendations that are supported by the findings
Recommendations
Bibliography, references, and resources

Feasibility Study

A feasibility study evaluates the desirability and practicality (feasibility) of a project, product, or decision. Before time and money are invested, businesses need to know the likelihood for success of the project.

Feasibility Study
Introduction to the project, product, or decision being investigated
Discussion of evaluation tools and methods
Presentation of findings
Discussion of feasibility
Recommendations
Bibliography, references, and resources

Strategic Plan

Strategic, tactical, and operational plans are included in this formal document that presents goals, means for achieving these goals, and calendars detailing when each goal will be achieved. Strategic, tactical, and operational plans present current management's recommended actions for the foreseeable future as well as a mission and vision.

Strategic Plan
Environmental Analysis—profiles of present and forecasted environments
Competitive Analysis—SWOT—Include all competitors
Mission—your organization's purpose today
Vision—your organization's purpose in the future
Strategic Plans—grand strategies including how, when, and costs purpose
Strategic Objectives—link mission to vision; financial, customer, operational
Tactical Plans—long range goals stating how, when, and costs
Operational Plans—short-range goals stating how, when, and costs
Implementation—a detailed plan for implementing
Evaluation—measures, monitors, and tracks whether you are achieving your strategic plan
Control—describes how you will make changes
Bibliography, references, and resources

Business Plan

The goal of a business plan is to persuade the readers into agreeing with your ideas. Usually, you are attempting to get something, such as money, equipment, or help.

Business Plan
Executive Summary—includes the highlights of everything below
Company Description—includes history, start-up plans, uniqueness
Product or Service—describes what you are selling, focuses on benefits
Market Analysis—identifies your market and customer needs
Competitive Analysis—identifies your competitors—SWOT
Strategy and Implementation—includes dates and budgets
Management Team—identifies and describes key management member
Financial Analysis—pro forma profit and loss and cash flow
Bibliography, references, and resources

Business Proposal

A proposal is usually created in response to a request for proposal (RFP). The proposal should include all topics listed in the RFP and present your offer in the best light as well as outline what you are offering. A good business proposal will persuade someone to accept your offer and will protect you by defining exactly what actions you will take.

Evaluation Report

An evaluation report is a systematic and impartial examination of actions or processes within an organization. This type of report does not make recommendations for change; it just states what is happening at the time of the report.

Synthesis Report

A synthesis report is an analysis of a series of evaluation reports to form an overall picture and assessment of the projects, policies, or programs that have been evaluated.

Assessment/Audit Report

An assessment report can be internal or external. Included in the assessment are internal reviews, impact assessments, monitoring activities, policy reviews, and operational research. Audit reports focus on what improvements can be made. These reports are written as factual and nonjudgmental.

Technical Report

A technical report provides needed information clearly and in an easy-to-read format. Technical reports focus on solutions to problems, not on the problems.

Follow-up Report

After the implementation of a new policy or project, procedure, hardware, software, etc., the follow-up report outlines the effectiveness of what was implemented. Desired changes are also included.

Press Release

A press release announces a newsworthy item. It should include all the relevant information about the story, such as who, what, where, why, when, and how.

Miscellaneous

Other types of writing include procedure manuals, operating instructions, announcements, and documentation. Many similarities in format exist in the various types of writing.

Format Styles

Format choices will be examined next. All writing should be attractively produced in an easy-to-read format. Requirements may be even greater if the writing is to recommend or persuade. The facts and figures are of no value if the intended audience never reads it.

The value of a good format is that it gets the attention of the receiver and makes the task of reading easy. Formats may include e-mail, memo, letter, form, or report. However, the writing can be produced with variations as a newsletter, brochure, magazine, booklet, manual, or social media.

The production techniques in Chapter 6—Producing apply to all of the format styles. However, some details on newsletters and brochures are included in this section.

E-mail, Memo, Letter

Many written communications need be nothing more than an e-mail or memo. The memo heading can be the company stationery provided for memos. Such stationery is intended for use in communicating with people within the office or company. In contrast, a letterhead is normally used if correspondence is with someone outside of the company.

You can save time by creating a personalized signature for an e-mail or a template for a memo. Advantages of creating a signature or template of your own can be twofold: (1) you will not need to rekey your own identification information each time you write an e-mail or memo, and (2) you can use a design or logo, including a photo or clip art, that attracts favorable notice.

An e-mail, memo, or a letter may be the appropriate vehicle for communication. If the writing is longer than two or three pages, however, you may find it better to use the memo or letter for a cover message to go along with the longer project. This cover message could be kept short but is effective in introducing or explaining the attached or enclosed communication.

If the contents can be included in a short e-mail, memo, or letter, you can still take advantage of the production features suggested in Chapter

6—Producing. For instance, side headings, bold and larger font sizes, color, and graphics, can be used. Such devices make the information more attractive, resulting in easier reading or scanning.

Form

Many times, writing is just completing a form. If the form is in an electronic format, you have the advantage of being able to key in the requested information.

If you cannot get an electronic copy of the form, you may want to take the time to replicate the form by scanning or keying it into your computer. Even though these tasks are time-consuming, it may be worth the effort—particularly if using the same form is going to be needed again in the future.

Report

A report does not have to look like an old-fashioned manuscript. By applying the production techniques discussed in Chapter 6--Producing, a report can look like a magazine article or an annual company report.

Variations allow more space on either the right or left side, side notes, and illustrations. The advantages of these techniques are readability. Also, blank space is available for the reader to scribble notes or make additions or corrections if desired.

Newsletter

The goal of a newsletter is to communicate information to readers. A typical newsletter is printed to provide news to a special group.

If the special group may be people within an organization, the newsletter then becomes a communication device allowing information to flow either upward to management or downward to the employees. The special interest group may be individuals outside of a company who are concerned with a special topic, such as members of a professional organization or a hobby club.

Newsletters are published on a timely basis, such as weekly, monthly, quarterly, or yearly. A challenge in designing a newsletter is to develop a format and general identifying look and, in addition, make each newsletter unique. Software is available to provide templates and/or ideas.

Newsletter Tips
Develop a logo, nameplate, or flag for the title—usually on the first sheet either at the top or left edge.
Create a heading listing the editor(s) and any others responsible for the publication along with their addresses, phone numbers, etc.
Choose desired column and type sizes—if narrower columns, use a smaller type size.
Keep text readable—usually defined as seven to ten words on each line.
Add interest with graphics and art—a good idea is to break monotony by using text-wrap techniques around the art.
Choose a thickness for lines that neither overpower nor get lost.
Consider allowing space for applying a label and sending as a self-mailer without an envelope.

Brochure

A brochure is a flyer, leaflet, or small pamphlet and is used in almost every area of business and education. A common use of a brochure is an announcement appropriate for advertising a meeting or a product. However, it can also be used to create a brief informative communication. A well-done brochure presents a lot of information in an attractive manner. For example, a brochure may contain an announcement of a product or a meeting, educational material, or a persuasive message.

Information on a brochure can be printed on both sides of a sheet of paper. Although the paper can be any size, standard 8½ x 11 paper or legal 8½ x 14 paper are the most frequent choices. Either a portrait layout (vertical) or landscape (horizontal) layout is possible. As in the case of a newsletter, software provides many templates to use in designing brochures.

Brochure Tips
Be sure the information is complete—when, where, why, who, and how.
Create a masthead listing the editor(s) and any others responsible for the publication along with their addresses, phone numbers, etc.
Keep the information simple.
Include appropriate graphics and visuals to make the brochure attention getting.
Select a small font size for the body text and vary the font sizes on other text to make the important information stand out.
Make some of the information into bullet listings or enumerations, boxes, tables, etc.
Use one of the panels to make the flyer into a self-mailer so that an envelope is not needed.
Purchase color designed paper and plan the brochure around the design on the paper or create your own design.
Purchase brochures pre-scored for folding or even containing a business card that is perforated and can be removed by the reader.

Magazine, Booklet, or Manual

The main difference between a newsletter or brochure and a magazine, booklet, or manual is that the latter groups contain more pages. Magazine, booklet, or manual are terms used somewhat interchangeably and could be considered in the book category. In fact, the techniques mentioned under newsletters also apply in this category; however, the page size may be reduced to standard book sizes.

Social Media

Social media is evolving rapidly and becoming an integral part of life online as social websites and applications proliferate. Social media is dedicated to collaboration, interaction, content-sharing, and community-based input. In business, social media is used to market products, promote brands, connect to current customers and foster new business.

Social media includes social networking, social bookmarking, social entertainment, social news, microblogging, forums, and wikis. The following chart provides examples of some of the popular social media cites and their goals.

	Social Media Cites
Facebook	The most popular free social networking website that encourages users to create profiles, upload photos and video, post and send messages to friends, family, business associates, and clients.
LinkedIn	A social networking site designed specifically for the business community. The goal of the site is for members to establish networks of professional people.
Google+	Google's social network, designed to imitate the way people interact offline better than other social networking services.
Twittter	A free microblogging service where members can post 144-character messages called tweets. Hashtags (#) are used to describe the tweet's content.
Wikipedia	A free, open content online encyclopedia created through the collaborative effort of a community of registered users. Anyone registered users. Anyone registered can create an article for publication.

Reddit	A social news website and forum where stories are socially curated and promoted by site members. Hundreds of sub-communities exist. Each has a specific topic such as technology, politics, or music. Content is voted on by other members. The goal is to get stories to the top to the top of Reddit's main page.
Pinterest	A social curation website for sharing and categorizing images found online. Description of the images are required, but the main focus of the site is visual. Clicking on an image takes the reader to the original source.
Instagram	One of the most popular image-sharing social networks. You just snap or upload your photo/video, apply quick edits, add a caption, tag it, and post it.
Snapchat	Snapchat is a mobile-only social network that features private messaging with photos and short videos that disappear within a few seconds of being viewed. It also has public stories that can be posted for up to 24 hours.
Tumblr	Tumblr is a popular blogging platform that has a huge community and a very visual appeal to it. Users can easily publish new posts, interact with each other, reblog posts, and even customize their mobile header. It can be used on the web or on a mobile device.

As with any written communication, you should use common sense and good judgment when posting on social media. Be sure to familiarize yourself with the accepted practices for the particular cite you plan to use. A few Tips for Success with Social Media are listed in the next chart. This list is by no means comprehensive.

Tips for Success with Social Media
Be positive
Use analytics
Be respectful
Don't pick fights
Be timely about posting

Separate opinions from facts
Contribute value-added information
Choose the right platform and interact often
Don't try to use more cites than you can keep with
Build social media into your business or personal plan
Respect intellectual property rights and copyright laws
Your first impression may be all you get—make it a good one
Don't send out invitations to play games or other timewasters
Include appropriate graphics and visuals for attention-getting posts
Grammar matters—always check grammar and spelling before posting
STOP! THINK! POST! Don't post when intoxicated, tired, angry, or upset
Assume all posts will be seen by future employers and current or future clients

Blogs

In the Information Age of the 21st century, people turn to the internet for information. Mobile devices and computers are constantly used to obtain answers to questions, or to find ways to improve our lives. Blogs help provide these answers and methods.

Blogs are online journals that provide information to the digital society. Blogs in various forms have been around for 30 years. However, the term Blog was first used by Peter Merholz in 1999; he combined the words "web log" into "weblog" and then separated them into "we blog" and then "blog" (Merholz).

Blog Growth
# of blogs double every second
173 thousand created every day
5 million created every month
62 million created every year

Blogs provide information on every topic imaginable. When individuals and businesses realized their importance to marketing, connecting with clients, and making money (the top-paying blog in the United States makes $14,000,000 a month); blogs really took off.

Over 437 million blogs existed in March 2018. If you lined up all people in the United States and Mexico, they still would not equal all the blogs in existence. The number of blogs in the world doubles every second. or 173 thousand blogs are created every day (Gaille, 2014). So, about 5 million blogs are created every month and 62 million are created every year.

Reasons to Blog

Individuals, organizations, and businesses have found numerous reasons to create and use blogs. The reasons for blogging are as varied as the topics that blogs cover. One of the main reasons for blogging is that you have something to say and a blog provides a place for you to say it. Additional reasons are listed below

Reasons to Blog
Help People
Build trust with your customers
Have fun and show your creativity
Establish your expertise and credibility
Interact with people with similar interests
Sell, market, or promote any product or service
Share your thoughts and opinions about a topic
Make a difference in the community, state, world
Stay connected with friends, family, and acquaintances
Remain active or knowledgeable in a field or subject area
Keep customers and clients up-to-date on news, deals, and tips
Generate income from selling products or services or advertising
Inform people, organizations, or communities about various topics

Starting a Blog

So, you want to start a blog. You have identified several reasons to create a blog, and whether you plan to use a blog creator, wed design company, or create your own, the list below provides a few tips.

Starting a Blog
Quality is King—Grammar, style, punctuation are all important. Use this book!
Fresh Content is Important—Update at least 3 times a week
Backlink, Backlink, Backlink—Link to new pages and build relationships, Google Analytics can let you see search terms that bring you traffic.
Meaningful Topics are a Must—Add value to your readers with how to guides, do's and don'ts, news topics, funny topics, health topics, and so on.
Passion About the Topic is Essential—If you are not passionate about the topic your readers won't be.
Common Keywords Should Be Used—Integrate industry-wide words
Hosting a Blog is Not Easy—Plan on spending a great deal of time for a successful blog
Don't Expect Immediate Results—It takes time to attract readers and more time to keep them coming back
Don't Do It Just for the Money—Many blogs never make money. On the other hand, many successful blogs make a lot of money.

Good Luck with starting your blog. And, if you want additional help with any aspect of your blog, simply search for blogs that will help you. If you don't find the right one, maybe that is one you should create!

Gaille, Brandon. Some Interesting Facts About Blogs August 2013, https://www.wpvirtuoso.com/how-many-blogs-are-on-the-internet/.
Merholz, Peter . Jump up^ (1999). "Peterme.com". The Internet Archive. Archived from the original on 1999-10-13. Retrieved 2018.

Parts of a Report

The parts of a report will vary according to its specific aims and purposes. An overview of all the various parts that can be included, along with an explanation of when and why the various parts should be used, is discussed next.

Executive Summary/Abstract

An executive summary or abstract of the report states in approximately a page or less a synopsis of the entire report. In the business world, an executive summary is extremely important. The executive summary may be read and used to judge whether the report is worth reading. On the other hand, the executive summary may be effective in helping the reader make a favorable decision before reading the rest of the report. Consider your report successful if this happens! Possibly because of its overall look of attractiveness and efficiency, your report portrays a confidence that leads to acceptance.

The executive summary or abstract should state the report in a nutshell—generally, it could include the purpose or objectives of the report, background, procedures or approach to the report, findings, and summary, recommendations, and conclusions.

A title page provides identification for the report. A typical title page could include information such as the following:

Title

Author or Authors

company, email address, phone number of the author(s)
if needed

Date

Purpose

prepared for whom and why if needed

Appropriate graphics always adds to a cover page. For example, adding a company logo (if you have permission) is effective in a report.

Contents

Because *Table of Contents* is a redundancy, it can also be referred to simply as *Contents*. Any report more than three or four pages long can benefit from the inclusion of a contents page. Thus, the formats of e-mail, memos, letters, or forms would not require a contents page.

Contents should appear at the top along with the headings and subheadings and the page numbers where they appear. Worded another way, the contents page is an outline; however, Roman and Arabic numbers used in the typical outline should not be included unless they are used in the report. A reference manual may include a more detailed numbering system to help in locating a specific section.

Leaders (dots or dashes) are used to help the reader follow the text to the page numbers. Your software may have an automatic way of inserting the leaders. Some programs even include a way of automatically generating the contents page. Only the page number where the topic begins is listed. The introduction is always on page 1. For example:

Introduction.....................1		Introduction.....................1-2
Related Research.............4	not	Related Research.............4-6

A contents page may include all levels of headings or may be restricted to only one or two levels. In developing a contents page, remember, the purpose is to provide an overview of what the report includes and to allow readers to locate and read only specific sections.

Introduction

An introduction tells the reader(s) the purpose and the background. The introduction should not include the findings or conclusions. The introduction always starts on page 1. Any pages before the introduction, such as the title page, contents page, or list of figures are normally not numbered.

Body

The body may contain a variety of different parts to fit various situations. The generic outline presented next probably sounds similar to a term paper or thesis assignment from school, but it provides some useful guidelines.

> Introduction
> Related Research
> Procedures or Methodology
> Findings
> Summary, Recommendations, and Conclusions

Appendices

An appendix (singular) or appendices (plural) contains supporting material to the report. The plural form can also be spelled appendixes. This supporting material might include longer information that may be needed for verification or backup information but might distract from the normal reading flow. Examples are listings, statistics, quotations, etc. Items in an appendix should be referred to at the appropriate place in the report as Appendix A, Appendix B, etc., and placed in the order that they were mentioned.

Bibliography/References/Resources

Although frequently used interchangeably, bibliographies, references, and resources are not exactly the same thing. A bibliography contains a list of writings on a subject. References are used to list citations made. Resources indicate where additional information on a subject can be found.

CHAPTER 2

Starting

> **Starting can be the hardest part!**
> *You should start by planning, researching, and outlining—steps that are all crucial in creating high-impact writing. Developing a detailing outline is critical for a success!*
>
> —Rhodes and Kupsh

The first step in writing is choosing the topic. Sometimes the topic is assigned, which brings you a step closer to getting the project underway. If possible, always try to have a topic of interest to you. The writing process will be easier and more beneficial if you are interested in the topic.

After selecting the topic, the next difficulty in writing may occur. It is called writer's block. Often, this block is caused by starting to write without proper planning, researching, and outlining. These steps are most important in creating a proper foundation prior to beginning the actual writing process. If you have a detailed outline, the topics in the outline become your headings and subheadings, and you simply write something under each heading and subheading.

Planning

A plan consists of a detailed scheme or method worked out in advance for the accomplishment of an objective. The steps in forming a plan involve a systematic approach to the writing process. The steps can be divided into the following categories: analyzing the target audience, setting up a time schedule, collecting the data, and establishing an organized overall plan.

Purposes or Objectives

When considering the topic, always begin by determining the purpose and/or objective. Sometimes it helps to think of a writing project in terms of solving a problem. Thus, the purpose or the objective is to address the problem.

Problems to be solved may include meeting a need for more information on a particular topic, an analytical look involving interpretation and/or recommendations, or a persuasive pitch to generate action. Chapter 1— Organizing lists examples of writings that fall into different and various classifications that tend to build one upon the other. For example, a persuasive communication will no doubt include information, interpretations, and recommendations, along with persuasive arguments for accepting or rejecting those recommendations.

Writing the problem statement is one way of beginning. The task of writing the problem statement is helpful in keeping both the writer and all subsequent readers in focus on the reasons for creating the writing.

The topic or issue, also referred to as a problem statement, should be supported by listing purpose(s) or objective(s). While a problem statement explains what, purposes or objectives explain why. If the writing project has more than one problem, purpose, or objective, plan to list each of these separately. Careful planning, analyzing, and organizing allow you to provide a clear and concise problem statement as well as goals for your target audience.

Target Audience

If you are writing for a target audience, an analysis of that target audience is necessary in the planning stage, the following questions may prove helpful in completing this task.

Analysis of the Target Readers
What is the educational level of the intended readers?
How much background or technical experience do members of your intended reading audience have on the topic?
Is the writing an upward, downward, or lateral communication device?
What is the age level, gender, and nationality for most of the readers?
Will the audience be expecting the writing to be formal or?
Is the writing one of many, or will it be one of a kind?
Is the writing expected by the readers?
What type of action—a verbal response, a written reaction, or an interview—do you anticipate from the audience?
Are you addressing the appropriate audience?

These questions are not a complete list but are merely intended to start thinking regarding the analysis of your target audience. An essential requirement is that you have a clear understanding of the target audience to focus on their needs.

Time Schedule

Creating anything new takes time—frequently, far more time than anticipated. A detailed timeline should be established to estimate the time necessary to complete the project—particularly if you have a completion deadline for the writing.

Establishing a timeline that involves estimating the amount of time needed for each of the different steps—as well as a breakdown of time needed for work within those steps—has several merits. First, the estimate provides a step-by-step schedule to follow. Second, it establishes projected daily or weekly goals rather than one final deadline. One bit of advice that many people find useful is to set an early deadline to leave extra days or even a week to take care of unforeseen problems. A simple Gantt chart shows a graphic presentation of a timeline.

#	Task	Who	Start	End	Dur	October	November
	Case Analysis		10/1	11/30	61		
1	Select Partner	Me	10/1	10/5	5		
2	Choose a Company	Both	10/5	10/10	5		
3	Reference Manager	Me	10/5	10/10	5		
4	Initial Research	Both	10/10	10/20	10		
5	Outline the Case	Both	10/20	10/21	1		
6	Gather all Data	Both	10/21	10/30	9		
7	Store References	Both	10/20	11/25	35		
8	Write Case	Both	10/30	11/25	18		

Even if the intermediate deadlines are not always met, a timeline will provide an indication of where you stand. Many people find that a timeline with incentives (such as a candy bar, television, or a movie) for completion can be an effective motivational device.

Overall Plan

A likely procedure in testing a new product by a company would be to have a time schedule, expectations, definition of tasks, definition of acceptance levels, etc. This overall plan would serve the purpose of putting everyone on the same page with the same agenda—important to the success of the test.

Similarly, a written overall plan should be prepared for a written project to show commitment and your plans to achieve that commitment. Such a plan may be required by your superiors; but even if it is not, it is important as a means of reiterating your goals and purposes and organizing the project.

Researching

The writer seldom knows all of the information to be included. Usually a collection of some type of data is needed. Data collection for consists of a scholarly or scientific investigation or inquiry. Such research is considered to be either secondary research (also referred to as existing) or primary research (also referred to as original). This data may be gathered from a variety of sources.

Secondary Data

If someone else has already completed an investigation and has documented the information, you can use that information as secondary data in support of the points that you make. Always use proper reference techniques as addressed in Chapter 4—Referencing. Secondary sources include information from scholarly journals, trade journals, books, magazines, or other publications.

Start the search for secondary data by using your library's database and article search. In addition to materials found in a library, computerized databases are a good source for locating information on a given topic. These databases are available in a number of commercial online services, such as Google Scholar. Also, most libraries subscribe to one or more specialized data search programs. Talking to a reference librarian can save time and improve the quality of your research. Reference management software often will import references directly from online databases.

Primary Data

Primary data includes data that you have personally obtained and compiled. Methods used to compile original data include surveys, experiments, interviews, focus groups, and testing.

Surveys are conducted through written questionnaires, interviews, or observations. Experiments test one method against another. In either a survey or an experiment, a research design should be developed. A research design includes details such as sample size, sampling techniques, procedures, and statistical methods used. When conducting original research, a book on research design could be consulted to determine proper methodology and statistical techniques for your project.

Outlining

Outlining is a vital step in organizing a written project. Organization is the process of putting something together as an orderly, functional, and structured whole; outlining is the best means of achieving this objective.

Preparation

Before developing an outline, you may find it helpful to record random thoughts and phrases about your topic—an exercise called brainstorming. The next step is to begin to cluster these random thoughts into logical groups. Many word processing programs contain an outline feature, which you may find helpful. However, your tablet, phone, computer, or notepad is sufficient and effective for developing an outline during the brainstorming stage.

Outline Requirements
A complete, organized list of what is to be covered in the writing.
Topics and subtopics using parallel construction of words within the different levels showing a breakdown of what is to be covered.
Descriptive and functional topics and subtopics rather than attention-getting ones.
The inclusion of two or more points within each subtopic.
A parallel hierarchy of topics and subtopics.
A logical or sequential arrangement of topics and subtopics—alphabetical by size (largest to smallest or smallest to largest), by time, etc.

If possible, involving other people may be a good way to provide more ideas and thoughts. You can do the initial brainstorming and clustering before submitting a draft to another person or persons. Or, you may want to involve others in the initial brainstorming process.

Evaluation

Creating high-impact writing does not totally depend upon the topic. For instance, a high-impact essay, resume, or report that is favorably received and generates action. To accomplish these goals, the writing must be carefully and thoughtfully designed during the initial preparation stage. Remember, the longest trip can be shortened by good planning that steers you in the right direction. A well-prepared outline is the first step in the right direction.

CHAPTER 3

Referencing

> *Plagiarism is a crime!* Failure to reference sources properly results in plagiarism which is stealing. Referencing a source can provide your written work with the words of an expert and give more authority to your writing.
>
> —Rhodes and Kupsh

Using the words and ideas of an expert adds credibility to your writing and shows that you have thoroughly researched the topic. Not only is it acceptable to use the words, ideas, and graphics of others in your writing, it is encouraged. However, you must cite the reference for each source or you are plagiarizing. Remember plagiarism is a crime like stealing.

People in all areas of business, education, and government are not only being fired for plagiarism, but many are paying fines or even going to jail. Plagiarism—whether it is accidental or intentional—is no longer tolerated. Anytime you use the words, ideas, graphics, or music of another (regardless of whether you have paraphrased the other work), you MUST include the name of the author, title of the work, when and where it was published—in other words cite the reference. This section provides you with methods that will help you avoid plagiarism as well as practical tips about the various types of referencing!!

Plagiarism

Written communication skills are valued in every profession. This fact has caused schools to incorporate writing assignments in almost every class. However, plagiarism is an epidemic in schools and in industry. On the job, employees may be demoted or fired for any type of plagiarism. In schools, students are suspended, and faculties are fired for plagiarizing. Unfortunately, in today's world of copy and paste, many people do not understand what constitutes plagiarism.

Common Forms of Plagiarism

The Writing Studio at Colorado State University (https://writing.colostate.edu/guides/page.cfm?pageid=313&guideid=17) specifically lists common forms of plagiarism.

- Purchasing an essay or paper from a web site (or anywhere else) and calling it your own.
- Borrowing another student's paper from a previous semester and calling it your own.
- Having someone else do your work, for free or for hire. Agreeing to do someone else's work is equally wrong.
- Claiming originality regarding material copied directly from outside sources. In other words, deliberately failing to cite sources.
- Improperly documenting quoted, paraphrased or summarized source material.
- Extending the length of a bibliography to meet project requirements by including sources not used in your research or making them up all together.
- Killing two birds with one stone. Recycling an essay or paper written for one class by using it in another class studying the same or similar material.

- Receiving help from other students on an essay or paper and turning it in under your own name as individual work.
- Collectively researching and writing a paper with other students and each turning copies into different class sections claiming it as individual work.

Avoiding Plagiarism

> Giving students a web-based tutorial on plagiarism is more effective in deterring the behavior than threatening students with detection and punishment. That's according to the results of an experiment conducted by professors at the University of Michigan and Swarthmore College . . . . The study, *Rational Ignorance in Education: A Field Experiment in Student Plagiarism,* found that incidents of plagiarism could be reduced by as much as 65 percent when students participated in a 15-minute Web-based tutorial that [taught them] what constitutes plagiarism and how to avoid it. (Nagel, *Campus Technology,* 2010)

The copy-and-paste features are valuable when writing. However, when you copy someone's words or ideas and then paste them into your writing, it is sometimes difficult to find the source later. It is better to copy the words into a notes software along with the complete citation. Always write the source on any material you collect. It is very frustrating to have a perfect quote that you cannot use because you are unable to locate the source. Reference management software is a great tool for organizing and citing your sources.

Don't plagiarize—it isn't worth it. You can use the words and ideas of another person; just say whose words or ideas they are with a proper reference. Some teachers run random sentences or a whole paper through one of the online plagiarism websites. Businesses and schools alike are taking plagiarism seriously.

Guidelines for Avoiding Plagiarism
Plan ahead and start early
Quote your sources properly
Keep sources in correct context
Don't save your citations for later
Keep your notes and your draft separate
Proper referencing of sources takes time
Avoid reading a classmate's paper for inspiration
Keep track of your sources; print electronics sources
If you cut and paste; file and label your sources carefully
Keep your own writing and your sources writing separate
Do not *buy* or *borrow* a paper from a web site, classmate, or a friend
Do not use a paper you wrote for a previous class in your current class
If paraphrasing or summarizing from another source, cite the reference
If using *ideas* of another, even if you change the words around, cite the reference
Don't wait until the last minute, effective writing and proper referencing takes time
Don't get in a desperate situation and say, "They probably won't catch it if I copy this."
If using the *exact words* of another, put the words in quotation marks and cite the reference

Citing Sources

Existing sources (secondary sources) may be integrated into your writing in three ways—*quoting, paraphrasing, and summarizing.*

1. *Quoting* (using the authors exact words) must be exactly as they appear in the original research.

2. *Paraphrasing* is restating the original source material in your own words.
3. *Summarizing* requires you to put the main ideas into your own words, while presenting a broad overview of the original.

All three methods require you to cite the original source. You have the flexibility of choosing any of the three; however, making use of all of them at different places may be the best solution.

If the majority of your paper is from existing sources, the information should be paraphrased or summarized. Avoid having numerous quotations that make your writing choppy and unprofessional. In general, you should have a minimum of ten different references in your paper.

Quotations, paraphrases, and summaries will prove valuable to you for the following reasons.

Value of Quoting, Paraphrasing, and Summarizing
Provides support for your ideas
Adds credibility and authority to writing
Allows the use of experts' words and ideas
Presents examples of several points of view
Refers to work that sets the stage for your writing
Highlights a point with which you agree or disagree
Indicates to the readers that the words are not just your ideas
Focuses on a prominent material by quoting the original author

Quoting

A quotation assures your readers that you have not changed the meaning. Quotations must match the source document word for word and must be attributed to the original author. In addition, it may also appear to be more authoritative. The fact that you are quoting information should be made obvious to the reader. A good rule of thumb is if you use *Copy* and Paste at any time, you *must* indicate that the text is a *quotation* by using quotation marks.

Quotations of 5 lines or more than 40 words should be set as a block quotation or set in from both margins by approximately 5 spaces or half an inch. When this is done, quotation marks are not used at the beginning or the end, though they may be necessary for some internal passages

Also, the insertion of personal comments and the indication of an omission are both possible in quotations. In a quotation, you may insert your comments between brackets.

Omissions from quotations are indicated by using ellipsis points—a series of three periods (. . .). If the ellipsis occurs at the end of the sentence, you need to use an additional point for the ending of the sentence—or four periods.

As previously noted, a quotation of less than 5 lines or 40 words can be included in the text by using quotation marks to distinguish it from your writing. If a quotation is more than a page or so in length, use only the most relevant portion or put material in summary form. Another alternative is to simply refer to the quote in the text of the paper and include it as an appendix. Conversely anything included in the appendix should be mentioned in the paper at the appropriate place.

Guidelines for Quoting
Refers to work that sets the stage for your writing
Highlights a point with which you agree or disagree
Quotations must match the source material word-for-word
Indicates to the readers that the words are not just your ideas
Focuses on a prominent material by quoting the original author
The fact you are quoting someone else should be made obvious

Use quotations marks at the beginning and end of the quoted material
Quotations of 5 lines (40 words) or more should be indented from both margins

Paraphrasing

Paraphrasing is restating another author's words or ideas in your own words. Paraphrasing passages rather than quoting passages may tie the work in better with your writing as well as take less space.

Even though quotation marks are not used when paraphrasing, a reader should always be able to tell exactly what is paraphrased and what are your own words and ideas. Statements that help when paraphrasing are as follows:

> According to Kupsh & Rhodes (2022)
> Kupsh & Rhodes (2022) state that . .
> Rhodes (2022) found that . .

Guidelines for Paraphrasing
Most of the material from other sources should be paraphrased or summarized
Paraphrasing includes reading someone else's ideas and putting the ideas in your own words
The paraphrased material is usually shorter than the original passage
When paraphrasing, the ideas or words belong to the original author, so you must cite the reference, or you are plagiarizing

Summarizing

When only the main, overall ideas from a source are needed, use a summary. Summaries present an abbreviated edition of the source's main ideas in your words. Summaries include stating only the main ideas of the source in your own words.

Guidelines for Summarizing
Most of the material from other sources should be summarized or paraphrased
Paraphrasing includes reading someone else's ideas and putting them into your own words
A summary can be as short as a few sentences or longer, depending on the difficulty of the source material and the degree of detail you wish to present
The ideas are still the author's, who wrote the words, and you must cite the reference, or you are plagiarizing

Technology-Based Tools

Writing and research can be time-consuming and difficult. Without excellent tools to help collect, save, and organize your information it is even more difficult. The following list provides the general areas where technology-based tools can help. A simple web search will reveal the specific names of tools for each area. The tips in the chart offer good advice in using technology-based tools.

Using Technology-Based Tools
Cites information
Annotates sources
Backups everything
Organizes your files
Synchronizes everything
Takes notes about your ideas
Keeps all your work in one place
Bookmarks/marks favorite web pages

Reference Management Software

One advantage of reference management software is the time users save inserting formatted citations into academic work. However, each user or group must develop a personal database of references. This process can itself be time consuming. Possible alternatives to reference management software are reference checkers, citation creators, and word processing software.

Reference Checkers

When using reference checkers, you do not have to develop and maintain your own database of references. Reference checkers take completed or almost completed papers and compare the citations listed with the references listed in the bibliography or references at the end. Inconsistencies between the citations and the reference list are then highlighted. Reference checkers claim to save you time because you don't have to compare your citations to your reference list. However, you must create and format the citations and the reference page.

Citation Creators

Citation creators or citation generators use online web forms to format citations and bibliographies according to specific style manuals such as APA—American Psychological Association, MLA—Modern Language Association, Chicago Manual of Style, and others. Some citation creators do not allow you to store any information while others store the citation data for later use.

Word Processing Software

Many word processing programs, such as Microsoft Word, include Reference sections that include the creation of contents, footnotes, citations, bibliographies, and tables. Using one program for everything can have its advantages.

Even though use of technology-based programs may be of help with writing, the writer must have a working knowledge of the various methods of citing references. In addition, only one method of citing references should be used.

Citing Sources

A variety of methods for citing sources is available. Three general methods are *parenthetical, endnotes, and footnotes.* While parenthetical is commonly used and easy for the reader, always consider your intended audience and any specific guidelines when choosing a method for citing sources. If a specific style is required, see the section Style Guides for more information. By reading your citation, the reader should be able to easily locate the exact original resource.

Parenthetical

Parenthetical references provide the advantages of footnotes and endnotes. They are easy for the writer to use and provide adequate, convenient citations within the text for the reader. In fact, this method is probably the easiest and also the most convenient for the reader.

In parenthetical references, a shortened reference is placed in parentheses within the text. A complete listing of these sources is then placed at the end of the section, chapter, or paper.

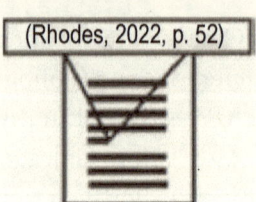

In using parenthetical references, place the last name of the author(s) and the date of publication in parentheses— separated by a comma. The name of a corporation, the name of a work, or some other means of identification may also be used with the date. The complete reference would be included in the reference page.

If the author's name is mentioned in the text, then you need use only the date in parentheses. If you refer to both the author and the date in the text, nothing needs to be put in parentheses; however, the reference should still be included in the alphabetical listing at the end of the chapter or paper. If the quote is from a specific page, you should include the page number in case a reader wants to locate the original writing.

Endnotes

Endnotes are indicated in the text by a raised number, though some systems may use a number in parenthesis on the same line as the text. The endnote eliminates the need for footnotes at the bottom of the page. Instead, a complete listing of the sources in numerical order is included at the end along with an alphabetized list of those same references. This method requires two lists but eliminates footnotes at the bottom of a page. The reader must turn to the back to identify the sources.

Footnotes

Footnotes are made by placing a raised number in the text at the end of the quotation—either direct, paraphrased, or summaries. Identification is then placed at the bottom of the page under a one-inch line. To identify a source, the reader must look at the bottom of the page.

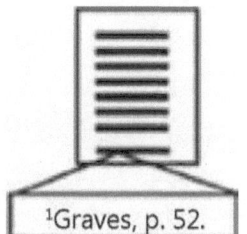

Using Style Manuals

Numerous reference styles are available depending upon your need. A more formal style is needed for collegiate writing, while a less technical approach is probably adequate for business and other needs. *American Psychological Association* (APA) publication manual is the most commonly used in business. *MLA handbook for Writers of Research Papers* is commonly used in schools.

Three popular style manuals are listed in the chart. For more details on each of these styles, you can search the web. A number of websites are available to provide details on how to cite various types of references. If you have specialized material to reference and cannot find an example, try to establish some logical arrangement. Remember to use common sense and to be consistent.

Popular Style Guides or Manuals
American Psychological Association (APA) Publication Manual
The Chicago Manual of Style
MLA Handbook for Writers of Research Papers by Gibaldi and Achtert

CHAPTER 4

Writing

> *Anyone can write. Developing an effective writing style requires knowledge and practice. The key is to write something that people want to read. This section provides an overview of the writing style techniques that can be most helpful.*
>
> —Rhodes and Kupsh

Writing style refers to the way ideas are expressed on the written page. Style can vary from one individual to another, reflecting the personality of the writer. Also, writing style can vary to fit a specific need or purpose.

With practice, you can improve your writing style. Consider how professional athletes practice to maintain and increase their skills. Writing is no different. Study and practice will lead to improved performance.

This section highlights the key techniques needed in developing a good style. The following techniques are discussed: *objectivity conciseness, coherence, tone, emphasis, variety,* and *readability*. Remember, this book is a survival guide for writing.

Objectivity

Writing requires a different style depending upon whether the objective is for the writing to be informal or formal. In general, essays, letters, memos, and social media involve writing your views and opinions while a report is based on facts rather than personal opinion and views.

Informal

Since informal writing is expressing "you," the approach is informal. Informal writing may either describe or serve as an argument but is your opinion/view. In general, the writing should be more informal using a personal approach with words such as *I, we, our, us, my, etc.* This informality still requires good writing as described in the chapters on starting, organizing, and polishing. If quoting or paraphrasing, the author and work should be referenced in order to avoid plagiarism, which is essentially stealing.

Formal

Reports require a more formal style and should be written from an objective standpoint. A report does not reflect personal emotions and opinions. Instead, a report includes facts and findings that ultimately lead to recommendations and conclusions formed on the basis of those facts and findings.

You can maintain an objective attitude by divorcing yourself from your personal biases and prejudices. You should look at all sides of the problem with an open mind before stating your conclusions. This role is similar to that of a referee at a sporting event or a judge presiding in court. Decisions are based on the results, the evidence, or an interpretation of the results and evidence—not on personal opinions and feelings.

Keeping an open mind when writing will make your conclusions and recommendations more believable. If a personal bias is revealed, the reader may question the accuracy of the report. The emphasis, therefore, should be on the factual material presented and the conclusions drawn rather than on any personal beliefs.

Objective writing is impersonal and does *not* use pronouns such as *me, my, us,* or *you.* Objective writing uses names (proper nouns) and may occasionally use *he, him, she, her, they,* and *them.*

Objective writing does not mean boring or dull writing. Most newspaper and magazine articles are written objectively. While some of them may be exciting and interesting, others may lack luster, depending as much upon the subject as the writing style. Thus, even the blandest of topics can be positively affected through a blend of *what you say* (content) and *how you say it* (written expression of ideas).

At times, of course, you may want to make your writing more personal. If the report is a personal communication between you and your associates, for example, you may prefer the more informal approach of using *I, my, me, we, our, us,* and *you.* Overuse of these pronouns, however, may make you sound conceited. Thus, you may want to limit personalization.

Before you start to write, decide which style—informal or formal—is better for your particular task. Deciding at the outset on which style is appropriate can save considerable time and effort during the editing process.

Conciseness

> "More is not always better, sometimes it is just more."
> (*Sabrina,* screenplay adapted by Barbara Benedek and David Rayfiel, 1995)

Conciseness is a necessity in today's busy world; it saves time and money for both the writer and the reader(s). Long written communications do not necessarily equal quality written communications. Important details can be lost. Teachers may do a disfavor by assigning their students a ten-page project when the information could be adequately stated in one or two pages.

The art of being concise is difficult. Conciseness is achieved in many ways. General categories of things to avoid in making your writing more concise follow.

Irrelevant Information

Information that is irrelevant should not be included. Perhaps the reader does not need to know everything you know on the subject. Everything included should be there for a reason and have a bearing on your topic and your purpose. A detailed outline helps eliminate irrelevant information.

Redundancy

Redundancy is the useless repetition of a word. Eliminate redundancy from your writing. Examples of redundancies are illustrated in the following list.

> 6 p.m. ~~in the afternoon~~
> ~~free~~ gifts
> ~~important~~ essentials
> ~~basic~~ fundamentals
> ~~personal~~ opinion
> ~~falsely~~ padded expense account
> ~~severe~~ crisis
> she ~~is a female who~~

Clutter and Clichés

Clutter and clichés are frequently combined in a way that wastes words. The following examples demonstrate ways of making writing more concise.

~~will you please arrange to send~~	please send
~~a check in the amount of~~	a check for
~~in accordance with your request~~	as requested
~~we are not in a position to~~	we cannot
~~reports that are long~~	long reports

Extra Phrases

Using hyphenated words (compound adjectives) helps reduce the number of words needed to express an idea. Note the following examples.

~~The writing techniques which are up to date~~
Up-to-date writing techniques

~~Reports written at the last minute~~
Last-minute reports

~~Avoid waiting until the last minute~~
Avoid the last-minute rush

Substituting a precise word or words for phrases eliminates extra words.

~~Tom was a teacher who was outstanding.~~
Tom was an outstanding teacher.

~~Writers create better output when they use a production package.~~
Writers using a production package create better output.

~~The report which is incomplete~~
The incomplete report

~~Paul waited in an impatient manner.~~
Paul waited impatiently.

Implied Ideas

Implied (obvious) ideas need not be restated. The following statements can be rewritten omitting words as shown.

~~She went to school and attended class,~~
She attended class,

He ~~took the test and passed it with high honors.~~
He passed the test with high honors.

~~Mary went shopping and bought a~~
Mary bought a

Abstract or General Words

On the other hand, using a single concrete word rather than a longer phrase will shorten the sentence but make the meaning somewhat vague. In reporting on the work ability of a person, words such as *dependable, efficient, nice,* and *superior* may sound good but tend to be hazy compared to more concrete descriptive words or sentences. For instance, you could cite specific examples for each of these words.

~~dependable~~	was never late to work
	was never sick
~~efficient~~	made deadlines
	won employee-of-the-month award
~~nice~~	gets along well with all employees
~~superior~~	made the highest score in a class of two hundred

Coherence

Coherent writing flows along without abrupt changes; or to put it another way, the writing sticks together. This cohesion is accomplished by linking the thought from one sentence to the next and from one paragraph to the next. Linking is done by repeating words and by using a transition.

Repetition

By repeating a word either directly or with a similar word, you will keep the reader aware of the topic. In the following examples, the addition of the word inserted in parentheses makes the writing stronger and clarifies the meaning. Without the inserted noun, the reader might be forced to reread the previous sentence to clarify what *this, that, these,* and those refer to or represent.

> This *(example)* will show
> That *(task)* is accomplished
> These *(papers)* will be delivered
> Those *(plans)* are the ones

Transition

Using transitions help to blend one thought with another, keeping the reader focused on the flow of the work. Transitions help the writing flow smoothly and bridge any gaps. Transitional words include explanation, enumeration or listing, similarity or contrast, and cause or effect.

Explanation. A transition is useful before giving an example. You can use such words as the following:

also	for instance
too	to illustrate
for example	in the illustration
as an example	as previously stated

Bullet Lists. A transition is useful before writing a list of items. You can list items using a numbered list. However, many times the number is not important, and the items can be listed using a symbol such as the following:

Thousands of symbols are available on word processing software or online, or you can use a photo to create a custom symbol.

If the items are short or special emphasis is not needed, you may prefer to list the items within the paragraph. This listing can be done by using the numbers: (1) first, (2) second, or () third. A semicolon should be used instead of a comma if the words in the listing include longer phrases using a comma.

Words within the paragraph are also effective in linking items. Examples are as follows:

in addition	third
first	next
second	finally

Similarity or Contrast. Transition words work effectively in showing either a similarity or a contrast between two situations. Some helpful examples are the following:

Similarity	***Contrast***
likewise	in contrast
similarly	in spite of
in a similar manner	on the other hand
by the same token	however
in the same way	on the contrary

Cause or Effect. Transitional words are also helpful in showing a cause or an effect:

because of
as a result
therefore
for this reason

Tone

The tone can convey a message to the reader(s). Care needs to be taken to assure that the right tone is projected. A neutral, unbiased stance is most convincing. Many different factors contribute to the tone of a message, such as using positive versus negative and active versus passive as well as bias-free language.

Positive versus Negative

People like to hear good news; therefore, you want to accentuate the positive and eliminate the negative aspect as much as possible. Exceptions can be made if you are consciously trying to dramatize a negative problem, but carefully analyze the negative statements to ensure that you are making the desired impression.

Some words automatically project a negative feeling or image. For instance, the words *delay, unable, cannot, inconvenient, disappointed, broken, not,* and *unfortunately* all create an *"oh dear, bad news"* effect.

If, on the other hand, you want to give a positive spin to bad news, use a more positive word.

Negative	*Positive*
~~do not forget~~	remember
~~you neglected to send~~	please send
~~cannot accept~~	unacceptable in present form

Active versus Passive

Writing in active voice—with the subject doing the acting—is usually a direct and dynamic method of writing. Yet, passive writing may be more appropriate at times. Here is an example of active and passive writing:

Active   John wrote the report.
Passive   The report was written by John.

Expletives

Expletives such as *there are, it is, it is noted that, it is understood that,* etc., should be avoided. Expletives are meaningless words used in beginning a sentence. Even though a sentence with an expletive may be grammatically correct, the sentence is unclear and may cause the reader to look back to find out what the expletive means. The following words may create interest in a novel but should be avoided in business writing.

Vague	*Definite*
~~there are~~	The report states . . .
~~it is said that~~	The research suggests . . .
~~it is understood that~~	The review indicates . . .
~~it is noted that~~	Furthermore, the results indicate . . .

Pronouns

Using a noun or the pronouns *he, she, him, her, they, and them* (writing in third person) is usually recommended for professional writing. Using the pronouns, *I, we, me, my, our, us,* and *them* (writing in first person) may seem to make writing more personalized, but readers may begin to think you are conceited after hearing words such as *I* or *we* too many times. Using *you* (writing in second person) is recommended for letter writing in an attempt to get the attention and interest of the reader.

You should carefully consider the desired impact *before* you start writing. Since a report is a factual account or summation of information, third-person writing may make the final result seem more businesslike.

Bias-Free Language

The tone of writing should never reflect a gender bias or any other type of bias—race, religion, age, disability, or ethnic group. Biased writing sends the wrong message and may alienate readers.

Stereotyping. If you refer to a man as a boss and a woman as a housekeeper, it is stereotyping. Avoid stereotyping by changing to plural form when possible and referring to both genders. Problems and suggested corrections are as follows:

> ~~The manager showed his appreciation~~
> The manager showed appreciation
>
> ~~The housekeeper is required to do her best.~~
> All housekeepers are required to do their best.
> He ~~is to report to~~
> He or she is to report to

Job Titles. Job titles and expressions can show gender bias. Eliminate the use of biased titles and substitute a more neutral word. Most words can be stated in a more acceptable version. For instance:

~~policeman~~	police officer
~~fireman~~	fire fighter
~~businessman~~	businessperson
~~working mother~~	working parent
~~foreman~~	supervisor
~~bag boy~~	bag person
~~stock boy~~	stock clerk
~~airline hostess~~	flight attendant

Emphasis

Words placed either first or last in a sentence receive the greatest emphasis. You should decide on your most important word or phrase and then decide whether you want that word or phrase to make an initial or a lasting impact.

In the following sentences, the attention is on Rodney in the first sentence. The second sentence places the emphasis on the report. If you want to give Rodney credit, place his name first. If the report being completed is more important, use the second sentence.

> ~~Rodney completed the report.~~
> The report was completed by Rodney.

Using either active or passive voice changes the emphasis of a sentence. For example, if you are portraying bad news, you may wish to write in a passive form to keep from sounding accusatory.

> ~~You neglected to include the data.~~
> The data was not included.

Variety

At times, writing rules seem to disagree. One rule will say to be parallel, and another rule will say to use variety. Both rules are correct, but each one has its place. The hard part is deciding when to be parallel and when to use variety.

In general, elements in a series—such as side headings, bullet lists, items in a series, or clauses—should be parallel. The following list provides examples of parallel writing as well as writing that is not parallel.

Variety is good in the length of sentences and paragraphs. Varying the length of sentences and paragraphs breaks the monotony for the reader. Too many short sentences may make the writing sound like a first-grader's. However, long sentences and paragraphs may put the reader to sleep. A combination will provide needed variety.

Another way of making your writing more interesting is to use variety in sentence structure. Simple sentences are easy to read but should be mixed with complex or compound sentences. Also, vary the pattern and begin some sentences with a prepositional phrase such as "During the winter" or a dependent clause such as "Because of the low budget." If applied correctly, variety does lend interest to your writing.

Comprehensive

Writing should be comprehensive, including all the necessary parts as mentioned in **Chapter 1—Organizing.** The recipient of the writing should be left with no unanswered questions and should not have to request additional data from the writer. A detailed outline usually insures that all the necessary topics have been included. The **Checklists** at the end of the book provide a way to evaluate your writing.

CHAPTER 5

Polishing

> **Polishing makes a report professional!**
>
> **The material included in this chapter was selected after analyzing common problems made by graduate and undergraduate students in the authors' classes.**
>
> **—Rhodes and Kupsh**

The image reflected by your work will influence your readers' reaction. Your work will be regarded as flawed and viewed with skepticism if it contains numerous writing errors—even if the work has a wealth of technical, scientific, and creative information.

Many people say they are interested in only the content—not how it looks or how well written it is! However, when faced with a stack of papers, all people are drawn to the ones that stand out. They are influenced by the appearance as much as by the facts and thoughts in the paper. Polishing your writing represents an extremely important piece of the writing puzzle. This section cannot possibly cover all there is to know concerning writing skills. However, the basics as well as many of the more common errors made by writers will be included. Topics included are abbreviations, acronyms, capitalization, italics, numbers, punctuation, spelling, and word division.

Abbreviations

Abbreviations should be used with caution. A few exceptions to this follow.

In general, the more formal your writing, the fewer abbreviations should be used. The following list illustrates places where abbreviations are commonly used.

- Titles before and after names

    Dr. Cruz
    Mr. Rhodes
    Mrs. Gray
    Ms. Rivera
    Drs. Rhodes and Kupsh
    Mary Buck, PhD or Ph.D.
    Nancy Merlino, EdD or Ed.D.
    Heather Gray, MD or M.D.
    Jim Scott Sr.

- Number when used with a figure   No. 24

- Companies and organizations with abbreviations used in letterhead   Brian and Co.

Acronyms

Acronyms—words formed from the initial letters of a name—of companies, departments, divisions, organizations, or agencies. Organizations can save a lot of space by using acronyms. Acronyms are so frequently used today that they have become an integral part of our lives.

Examples:	COD	NFL
	UPS	TMI
	RSVP	BFF
	IBM	ERP
	OSHA	NCLB
	FBI	MRP

However, if the readers are not familiar with the acronyms used, they may have trouble comprehending or following the meaning. One helpful rule is to always spell out the words of the acronym *the first time it is used*.

Examples:	Supply Chain Management (SCM)
	Enterprise Resource Planning (ERP)
	No Child Left Behind (NCLB)
	Material Resource Planning (MRP)
	Just-in-Time (JIT)

In addition, you can include a *List of Acronyms* on the page following the Contents. This inclusion allows the reader to easily look up the meaning of the acronyms.

SCM	Supply Chain Management
ERP	Enterprise Resource Planning
NCLB	No Child Left Behind
MRP	Material Resource Planning
JIT	Just-in-Time

Capitalization

A common dilemma is deciding when to capitalize letters and when to use lowercase letters. This dilemma may be one of the reasons many people tend to use all capital letters—thus avoiding the decision entirely. All uppercase letters are hard to read and should be avoided.

These guidelines provide a foundation for determining what to capitalize. Capitalize the first letter of:

- The first word of a sentence
  Capitalize the first letter of the first word in a sentence.

- The first word of a direct quotation
  The leader said, "Go do your work."

- The first word following a colon
  Do yourself a favor: Practice your writing.

- The names of specific things, such as

people	Andi Gray
days and months	Sunday, March
title of people	Aunt Nettie
	(but not without the name—my aunt)
president	the President
vice president	the Vice President
	(of the United States)
holidays	Thanksgiving
nationalities and races	German
languages	English
buildings and rooms	Business Building
lakes and mountains	Mono Lake
sections of the country	the West
	(but not directions)
ships and airplanes	Santa Maria
space vehicles	Discoverer
publications	Newsweek
books and articles	The Chicago Manual of Style
	(except for articles—a, an)

	(except for prepositions—of, to, in, on, for, etc.)
	(except for conjunctions—and, but, or, nor, etc.)
artistic works	Mona Lisa
epithets	the Big Apple
registered trademarks	Xerox, Kleenex
abbreviations	MBA
acronyms	BFF

Italics

Words and phrases are easier to read when italicized rather than underlined. Modern twenty-first century writers use italics to set words and phrases apart from the rest of the text.

Italics are useful to:

- Indicate names of books, magazines, newspapers, plays, and movies.
  Publication Manual of the American Psychological Association will help you prepare effective academic reports.

- Mix foreign words with English words.
  She said *"Buenos dias."*

- Place emphasis or highlight a word.
  She was *guilty*.
  Please *mark* the item that you want.

- Refer to a word as a word
  The word *rush* was not used.

Numbers

Extreme accuracy is important when using numbers. A writer must decide when to use a number as a figure and when to spell it out. A few basic rules to follow are listed.

- Numbers are spelled out for one through ten.
  The report surveys three companies.

- Figures are used for numbers larger than ten.
  The report surveys 50 companies.

- Numbers are spelled out when used as the first word of a sentence.
  Fifty years ago, this company began operations.

- Figures are used:
  - in a listing when one of the numbers is higher than ten.
    The committee consists of 3 men and 17 women.

  - to express dates without th unless the number is before the month.
    February 20   20th of February

  - to express sums of money.
    $15 million or $15,000,000

  - to express chapter and page numbers.
    chapter 5   page 7

  - to express decimals, percentage, dimensions, weights, and temperatures.
    .15 15% 15 x 0 15 pounds 80°

- Omit the decimals in even-dollar figures, unless other numbers in the same sentence include cents.
  The cost of the report is $15.
  The costs of the reports are $15.00 and $21.50.

- Use words to represent time when o'clock is used but figures with p.m. or a.m.

    eight o'clock   *8 p.m.*   *10 a.m.*

- Omit the minutes unless another time is used in the same sentence where minutes are needed.

    8 p.m. to 10 a.m.   *9:00 to 5:30*

- Use words for names of streets up to and including twelve.

    Third Avenue   *First Street*   *15th Street*

Punctuation

Punctuation used correctly adds clarity to writing; used incorrectly, it can confuse or even distort the meaning. The main types of punctuation are the *apostrophe, colon, comma, dash, diagonal, ellipsis points, exclamation, hyphen, parentheses, period, question mark, quotation marks, semicolon, and underscore*. A few general guidelines are reviewed for each of these types of punctuation.

Apostrophe

' The apostrophe shows possession. Use before the s if singular; use after if plural or if a word ends with s.

Paul's report
boy's car but boys' car (if two boys own one car)

' Indicates omissions in contractions and in dates.

She can't read the report today.
The company was founded in '53.

' Forms the plural of numbers, letters, and words.

Mind your p's and q's.
The report was full of or's and nor's.

WRITING: A SURVIVAL GUIDE

Colon

: Use a colon before a list of items or a series of words—whether listed in the sentence or on separate lines.

The following people are exempt: John, Robert, Edward, and Tom.

The following people are exempt:
  John
  Robert
  Edward
  Tom

: Use a colon when the second clause explains or clarifies the first clause.

Written communications are vital in the world of business: without them, more meetings would be needed.

Comma

, Use a comma to separate words, phrases, and clauses in a series.
Preparation consists of planning, writing, and editing.

, Use a comma between two adjectives.
The attractive, efficient paper . . .

, Use a comma to separate two main clauses.
The project is difficult, and the research will require several days.

, Use a comma to set off introductory phrases.
Frequently, the work requires . . .

, Use a comma to set off words, phrases, or clauses that interrupt a sentence.
The work, being completed by a committee, is . . .
She is, in my opinion, a . . .
The boss, Robert Smith, is . . .

Dash

- Use a dash to show an afterthought or a summation.
    > Refer to a piece of art before it appears—not after.
    > The staff—including clerical workers, managers, and executives—is to . . .

- Use a dash to indicate a sudden change of thought.
    > The report was due last week—but the workers were sent home.

Diagonal

/ Use a diagonal or slash or one of the two or both in the expression and/or.
    > Susan and/or Mark will write the report.

/ Use a diagonal or slash in fractions, with abbreviations, or with discount terms.
    > 6 2/3   c/o   2/10   n/30

Ellipsis

... Use an ellipsis to indicate the omission of parts of a quotation. If at the end of a sentence, use four dots—the period at the end of the sentence accounts for the fourth dot.
    > "The people will arrive . . . after the event."
    > "The people will arrive . . . ."

Exclamation Point

! Use an exclamation point to indicate excitement, emotion, or a command.
    > The end is near!

Hyphen

- Use a hyphen in compound surnames.
    > Rhodes-Rivera

- Use a hyphen to separate numbers such as in telephone or social security numbers.
    (909) 869-1000   512-34-0000

- Use a hyphen when two adjectives modify a noun.
    well-written book   first-rate hotel

- Use a hyphen in word division at the end of a line when lines fall short or are too long.
    (See Word Division rules.)
    profes- sor   knowl- edge

Parentheses

( ) Use parentheses to set off nonessential explanatory words, phrases, or sentences—the use is stronger than a comma but not as strong as a dash.
Please show your costs (lines 7-25).

Period

- Use a period at the end of a sentence.
    The meeting ended.

- Use a period in abbreviations and decimals.
    Dr.   Blvd.   5.8%

- Use a period to separate numbers in telephone numbers.
    512.34.5489

Question Mark

? Use a question mark at the end of any sentence asking a question with an answer expected.
When is the report due?

? Use a question mark in parentheses to express doubt.
The company was founded in 1980(?).

Quotation Marks

" " Use quotation marks to enclose a direct quotation. Periods and commas go inside the quotation marks; colons, dashes, and semicolons go outside the quotations marks. Exclamation points and question marks go inside the quotation marks if they are part of the quoted material and outside if they are not.
She said, "The air is bad."
Did she say, "The air is bad"?

" " Use quotation marks to enclose titles, words, or phrases borrowed from others or used in a special way.
The "Supply Chain Lab" is now open.
A "magic" atmosphere was created.

Semicolon

; Use a semicolon to join two independent clauses not separated by a coordinating conjunction such as and, but, or, nor, etc.
The work is completed; the report will be mailed next week.

; Use a semicolon to connect two main clauses using a conjunctive adverb such as *however, nevertheless, consequently, therefore, moreover, hence, and furthermore.*
The work is not completed; however, it will be mailed by the end of the month.

; Use a semicolon to clarify series of words and phrases requiring other internal comma punctuation.
The executive staff consists of John Johnston, President; Marcia West, Vice-President; Susan Martinez, Secretary; and Ron Smith, Treasurer.

Spelling

Correct spelling is imperative in any written communication if you want to create a favorable image. Spellchecks are available on software programs; however, the spellchecks are unable to pick up some types of errors.

The following list of words illustrates types of errors that would not be found by a spellchecker on the computer. You can use a regular dictionary or an online dictionary to be sure you have the right word.

accede	exceed
accept	except
access	excess
ad	add
adapt	adept
addition	edition
advice	advise
affect	effect
all ready	already
all ways	always
allowed	aloud
any way	anyway
are	our, hour
capital	capitol
cease	seize
cite	sight, site
complement	compliment
council	counsel
descent	dissent
desert	dessert
device	devise
disapprove	disprove
disburse	disperse
dual	duel

elicit	illicit
emigrate	immigrate
expand	expend
farther	further
foreword	forward
formally	formerly
forth	fourth
incidence	incidents
interstate	intrastate
its	it's
knew	new
later	latter
leased	least
lessen	lesson
maybe	may be
passed	past
personal	personnel
principal	principle
role	roll
stationary	stationery
suit	suite
than	then
their	there
to	too, two
weak	week
weather	whether

Word Division

Dividing words at the end of a line can be another difficult decision. Many word processing programs include a feature that will allow you to control the word divisions used.

WRITING: A SURVIVAL GUIDE

You may choose to manually control hyphenation (referred to as force hyphenate). Some of the programs will give suggestions on acceptable word divisions. However, be aware of a few general guidelines in making wise decisions on when, where, and how to divide.

A good rule of word division is *don't!* However, you may find that you must sometimes divide words to make lines end evenly on the right or, if using full justification, to prevent large spaces between words. You may even find, on occasion, that to have proper line endings you need to rewrite, rearrange, or restate your thought. If you must divide words, use the following guidelines.

Guidelines for *Not* Dividing Words
The first and last lines of a paragraph or a page.
More than two lines in a row.
Five or fewer letters.
Only two letters will appear on the next line. (such as in *careful-ly*) suggest *care-fully*.
Only one letter is left on the first line. suggest no division.

Guidelines *for* Dividing Words
Only between syllables—thus, one-syllable words cannot be divided.
Keep a single-vowel syllable with the first part of the word. such as *form-ulation*   suggest *formu-lation*
Do not divide a word of five or fewer letters. *cable   ideal   into   icon*
Divide compound words between the two words. *sales-person   desk-top*

CHAPTER 6

Producing

> **Producing** includes techniques needed to make your writing appealing to readers. The design elements of fonts, color, paper, layout, and graphics discussed in this chapter will provide you with ideas that will make your work stand out.
>
> —Kupsh and Rhodes

Today's technology makes it possible to create high-quality written work. No longer does your work have to look like a diary. Instead, it can look like a professional publication.

Fonts

In working with fonts, you need to consider the *classifications, kinds, size, spacing, alignment, and a variety of other characteristics*. The choices you make can greatly affect the impression your projects display—be sure that the impression is favorable and conveys the appropriate and desired message.

Classifications

The default font is frequently set and may be the one that ends up being the one used by most people. Many fonts may be appropriate and easier to read. Times New Roman used to be the default setting; even though it is still available, it makes your work look like it was completed on a typewriter. Different font styles can serve a variety of purposes. This book uses Calibri for the body and Franklin Gothic for the headings and subheadings.

Hundreds of fonts are available. Having the appropriate, distinctive font can make your project stand out. The classifications of fonts fall into four areas—*professional, formal, casual, and headings and subheadings.* The following lists consist of categories of fonts selected by the authors.

Professional Fonts and Headings/Subheading. These fonts are shown in size 12 and are appropriate for most projects. Research reports, case studies, feasibility studies, strategic plans, business plans, and business proposals would lend themselves to business professional fonts. Fonts may vary according to your software.

Professional Fonts
Arial
Arial Narrow
Arial Rounded MT Bold
AdobeGaramondPro
Adobe Caslon Pro
Calibri
Garamond
Kozuka Gothic Pro M
Tahoma
Tekton Pro
Verdana

Heading/Subheadings Fonts
Arial Rounded MT
Bodoni MT Black
Cooper Black
Elephant
Franklin Gothic Heavy

Formal Fonts. Formal fonts are appropriate for e-mail signatures, brochures, newsletters, and invitations. Be sure these fonts are large enough to be read easily.

Casual Fonts. Casual fonts are appropriate for e-mail signatures, brochures, newsletters, and invitations. Be sure these fonts are large enough to be read easily.

Casual Fonts
Chiller
Comic Sans MS
Hobo Std
Jokerman
Poplar Std
Snap ITC

Variations

A variety of decisions are needed when working with fonts. With good choices, these variations can make your writing have that extra "zing." A font usually means a complete set of characters *(the full alphabet, numbers, and symbols)* in one thickness and style. Fonts come in all the variations of a basic design in every thickness and size.

Plain, Bold, Italics, etc. These variations include bold, italics or oblique, bold italics, shadow, outline, and strikethrough. If used correctly, these features add not only to the attractiveness of a project but increase the readability.

Plain	Outline
Bold	~~Strikethrough~~
Italics	Underscore
Bold Italics	Glow

Condensed, Narrow, and Expanded. Many fonts are also available in condensed, narrow, or expanded versions. These variations are particularly helpful when the writer wants to say a lot in a small space or expand a few words to fill a larger space.

Thickness. The thickness of the strokes making up the letters is another choice affecting the size or look of a letter. Terms used to distinguish among the thickness of a font in a specific size are extra light, light, regular, medium, semi bold, bold, extra bold, heavy, or ultra-bold.

Uppercase and Lowercase. Printed materials using lowercase and uppercase are more distinctive and easier to read. Therefore, putting words, phrases, lines, or paragraphs in all uppercase letters tends to make the words harder to read rather than easier to read.

> ALL CAPS ARE HARD TO READ.
> Lowercase is easier to read.

Underscoring. Underscoring should be reserved for e-mails, web links, and hyperlinks. If you have the urge to underscore, avoid doing so; instead insert the shape of a line underneath the word(s) or put a box around the word(s).

Reverse Type. Headings in reverse type—white or light characters on a dark background—offer an eye-catching combination for headings. However, too much reverse type can become difficult to read.

Drop Caps. Another variation possible for the beginning of a chapter or a new section is the use of a drop cap. Note the drop caps in the example below as well as those used in this book.

> A drop cap is a good beginning for a chapter. The use of a drop cap makes a distinctive start for a chapter.

Sizes

Text can range from 2 points to extremely large sizes (see examples on the right). The logical size for text body ranges from 10 points to 12 points, depending on the particular font. Headings are normally made in bold and or italics to capture the reader's attention and can vary in size to show the level of importance. In general, the larger the letters, the more important the heading!

7 9 10 11 12 14 18 20

24 36 48

Line Spacing

Line spacing can be varied for a more pleasing look. Copy may be 12-point font size with 14 points of line spacing, or, as the illustration shows, 10 points with 15 points for more line spacing.

> This is an example of 10-point font using 15-point line spacing.

Alignment

Font alignment (left, right, centered, or justified) is possible either before or after the words are keyed into the computer.

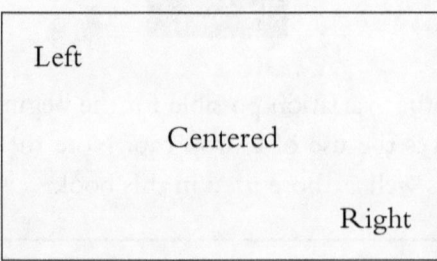

Justification, making both the left and right margins flush, gives a written project a blocked look and is preferred by some individuals. However, justification should not be used if it causes large blank spaces to run through the copy as shown by the arrows.

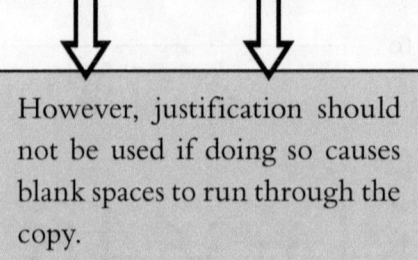

Hyphenating words, either through the software or by manually forcing words to be divided, can help to prevent large blank spaces and give the copy a tighter look. Hyphenation rules should be followed.

Uneven line endings provide a visual crutch for the eyes in addition to giving a more artistic look to the page. While research has shown that readability is improved if a ragged right margin is used, the written project with a right justified margin looks very professional. The choice is one for personal judgment.

Color

Color can be used for paper, covers, background, and fonts. Written documents do not have to be a black- and white-affair. Many projects, reports, and books are still printed with black ink on white paper. However, font colors can add to the attraction. Be sure that the font color used is dark enough to provide a good contrast with the paper.

If photos are to be included, a very white paper will show the light highlights better and make the dark inks seem darker. On the other hand, you may want to use paper that is slightly off-white (natural, cream, ivory, eggshell, mellow, or soft white) to reduce the glare. Also, the use of a light color can make a paper stand out from others in the stack, which is especially important if you are submitting a proposal where there is competition for a bid or a resume to get an interview with a company. Color is also useful in coding material.

Advantages of Using Color
Quick identification of sections
Glossaries or appendices to allow for easy referencing
Section or chapter heading of each new section
Covers and a neutral white, off-white, or beige for the inside
Fonts if they are dark enough to provide a contrast

Paper

Paper comes in different types, weights, and sizes. The quality of the paper reflects the professionalism of the project.

Type

Paper types include bond, matte, or glossy. A glossy paper provides a more sophisticated look and is better for halftones and color printing. Even without halftones, however, printing on glossy paper will be clearer.

> Some types of paper have a right side and a wrong side. Therefore, if only one side of the paper is to be used, printing should be on the right side. When you place the ream so that you can read the label, the right side of the paper will be on top.

Papers with a high rag or cotton content are more expensive but age better with less deterioration in color and context. Papers made without any rag content are more economical and good *only for papers* that will be read and sent to the recycling bin within a short time.

Weight

When paper is cut, the result is four stacks of 8 ½ x 11 sheets. Thus, the weight of four reams of paper represents the weight on the package. A twenty-four-pound weight is usually a good choice. If you are printing on both sides of the paper, you need to get a heavier weight and determine that the front side of the sheet does not bleed through to the back.

Size

Most writers assume that they will print on standard 8 ½ x 11-inch paper. However, many possibilities are available. Even if your printer accepts only standard- or legal-size paper, you are not held to these sizes because the paper can be trimmed to a desired size after printing.

Layout

Many considerations and decisions are required in creating a vision of the final document. These considerations are *page orientation, margins, column size, blank space, headings and subheadings, page numbers, headers and footers,* and *binding, and covers.*

Page Orientation

Page orientation is either portrait (vertical) or landscape (horizontal) and should be decided at the start. People tend to use portrait because they are used to it; however, a landscape orientation might work very effectively. Not all pages have to be the same. Using landscape orientation is very effective for displaying large spreadsheets or large pictures. Landscaped pages are displayed effectively when the top of the page is the binding side.

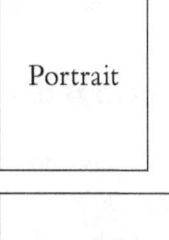

Margins

Adequate margins should be left to give each and every page a frame or border. Top and bottom as well as the left and right margins should all be even unless the document is to be bound. The amount of room left for the binding will vary according to the type of binding used—see later topic on binding. However, you must determine the type of binding desired before determining your margin settings. On a standard page of 8 ½ x 11, you will normally need to allow a quarter of an inch to a half inch of extra space for the binding.

Column Size

Research has shown that it is possible to read faster and comprehend more information when shorter lines are used. The actual length of the line will, of course, depend upon the page size. If you are using standard size (8 ½ x 11), you may want to consider using a columnar layout format. A columnar format works great for a business report, a newsletter, or a brochure. You want the reader(s) to find it easy and pleasurable to read—not dull and boring.

Blank Space

Blank space is very important for a professional look. Actually, each page should contain approximately 50 percent or more blank space. Pages with too much type and art give the appearance of being too heavy and hard to read.

Headings and Subheadings

Headings and subheadings are crucial in helping the busy readers of today. Effective writing requires headings and subheadings to help the readers keep focused. Remember that a reader may be interrupted with a phone call, visitor, or some other distraction—causing the mind to wander. Headings and subheadings can do wonders in helping to keep readers focused as well as allow readers to scan the copy for parts that are of special interest to them. Headings and subheadings can be used from the outline.

Guidelines for Headings and Subheadings

Make headings and subheadings concise but descriptive—possibly attention getting.

Follow parallel construction—verb and noun or nouns only.

Break the divisions down so that a heading or subheading always has two or more listings.

Make the headings and subheadings agree with the contents, although the contents may omit minor subheads and list only two or three levels.

A hierarchy of sizes and styles is needed for showing the various levels of headings or subheadings. The hierarchy style should be consistent and logical and progress from higher to lower levels in an obvious pattern. For instance, check the examples in the box.

> # First-level Subhead 18 Bold
> ## Second-level Subhead 14 Bold
> ### *Third-level Subhead 12*
> ### *Bold Italics Fourth-level Subhead Bold Italics Indented*

Page Numbers

Any time you have more than one or two pages, you need to number them. Software has the capability of performing this function automatically, but you must determine where you want the page numbers. Several choices are acceptable—either the upper or lower outside corners or the middle of the bottom of the page. Placing the numbers on the outside corners allows readers to locate a specific page more easily when scanning through a project.

Page numbers should start with the second page of the body. This page is numbered 2. The Title Page, Contents, and other preliminary pages are typically not numbered. More formal documents such as theses and dissertations may use Arabic numbers (i, ii, iii, iv, v, etc.) for the preliminary pages.

Headers and Footers

In today's busy world, readers frequently scan written material rapidly rather than reading it thoroughly from front to back. These readers are helped in locating or identifying a particular section or area if headers (identifying information at the top of a page) and footers (identifying information at the bottom of a page) are used. Headers and footers should not be confused with footnotes. Variations are possible, but one logical system is to have the left-facing page show the overall title and the right-facing page show the chapter or section title. Thus, a reader can quickly check the name of the document and also focus in on the specific subject.

Binding

Binding is that added step that can make a good first impression, as well as keep your work organized. Remember, the binding determines the amount of your left margin. The binding depends upon how many pages and the type of impression you want to make. Small papers of 20 of fewer pages can be stapled. Holes can be punched to place your work in a three-ring binder. Many other options are available with perfect, wire, or spiral binding being good choices. Be careful that you do not select a binding that will fall apart easily.

Cover

A customized cover can set your work apart from others. The cover can vary from ordinary title pages, to front and back pages using heavier paper, to specially ordered personalized notebooks.

Studies by General Binding Corporation show that a written project is twice as likely to be read and three times as likely to be saved if it is attractively bound.

Graphics

Anything on a page other than text is referred to as graphics. When used in a document, graphics should clarify, add to, illustrate, or enhance the document in some way. Line after line of text is boring and readers tend to skip over information. Graphics can improve readability. However, graphics should not be used without a specific reason or purpose. Otherwise, the inclusion of graphics may be distracting and confusing rather than helpful to your readers.

Illustrations may be labeled and referred to in the text. More formal documents may refer to any of the graphic illustrations as Figure 1 or Illustration 1 (followed with the title). The label can be above or below and left justified or centered. The labeling makes it easier for readers with the text saying, "as shown in Figure 1 . . ."

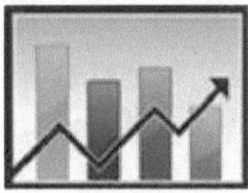
Figure 1—Yearly Sales

Lines, Boxes, Shapes, Background Tints, Patterns and Borders. *Lines, boxes, shapes, background tints,* and patterns are helpful in making documents more stimulating and appealing to readers.

The use of lines, boxes, and shading is helpful in creating divisions or focusing attention upon a given area. Icons or symbols available in various fonts may help focus or direct the reader's attention. Logos provide a subtle way of marketing your company or providing a theme for a product or topic. Additional graphics can include page borders and a watermark used as a background.

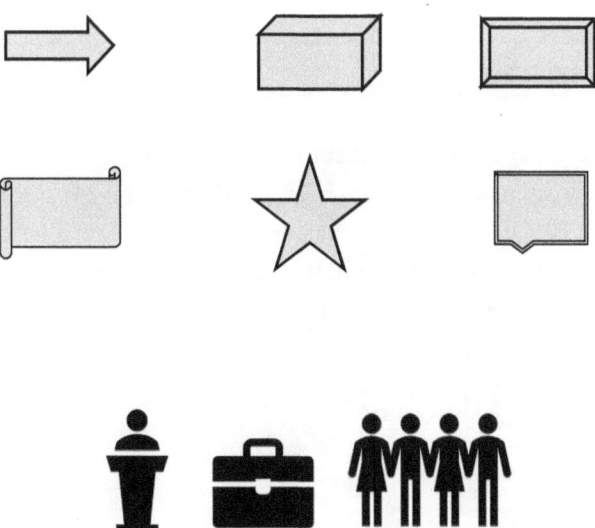

Photos and Clip Art. Photographs or clip art are available online. Or you can add your own original photographs or drawings. For instance, if you want a picture of a building, you can use clip art to portray the image. But if a real photo is available, you can project a more realistic image for the reader. Be sure to cite the source of the graphic or picture unless it is yours or not copyrighted.

Tables. Using a table to list items is a variation of bullet lists. For instance, if you want to show the various kinds of graphics, you could use a table similar to the one at the end of this chapter. You could have numerous columns as well as any number of row in a table, which makes for quick reading.

Types of Graphics
Lines, boxes, shapes, background tints, patterns, and borders
Photos and clipart
Tables
Charts and graphs

Charts and Graphs. Information containing and comparing numbers is easier to visualize in a chart or graph than when expressed in words only. Spreadsheets make information easy to display. The chart/graph below displays information on the skills needed for children to get ahead in the world today. Note that communication is 90 percent and writing is 75 percent.

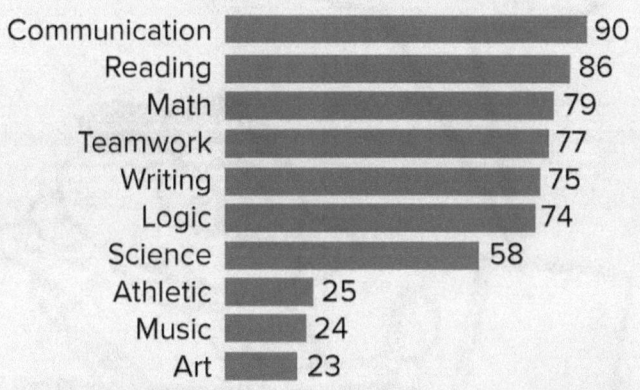

CHAPTER 7

Finishing

> *Think you are finished? Think again!*
>
> *All your hard work can be wasted if you do not follow through with the finishing touches.*
>
> —Rhodes and Kupsh

If readers see errors in the first few pages, your credibility may be lost, and the work is not read. An important aspect of any written project is accuracy and meticulousness. Little errors can make a big difference—the unfavorable kind. Therefore, the final step in finishing a written project is to edit and proofread your work carefully.

In addition to editing and proofreading your own work, ask other people to edit and proofread your work for you. You might want to assign them different tasks—like those performed by the staff in publishing a book. Editing and proofreading are needed to make sure that your writing is accurate as well as meticulous in its final form.

Editing

Three different types of editing are required for any type of writing—*substance, style, and consistency*. Even though these can be completed by you or another person, it may be better to think of these as separate activities. Trying to do everything at once is hard; most people have trouble completing three things at the same time.

Substance

Before giving your work a more detailed scrutiny, a general content look is needed. Questions under consideration during this editing process are as follows:

Editing Questions
Is the material complete?
Should any of the content be omitted?
Is the information correct?
Is the content presented in the right order?
Is any reorganization needed?

Style

Several types of style should be considered during the editing. First, is the writing consistent with the recommended styles described in **Chapter 4—Writing** and the style manuals for referencing discussed in **Chapter 2—Starting**? Next, have the styles or rules provided been followed properly? Some companies have their own corporate style guides. Teachers may also request a certain style.

Consistency

Another type of editing involves looking for consistency. Details in style should be consistent; possibly several ways are correct, but one way should be chosen and used throughout. If you are working with a team, proofing for consistency is very important. Other types of consistency are listed under the next section on proofreading.

Proofreading

Proofreading your own work is hard and not very efficient. Because you are so familiar with your own writing, you tend to race through and think of the bigger picture, the next assignment, the slides you need to make when you present your work, or whatever. Someone else who has not been involved in the writing can give it a much fresher and more efficient look.

In proofreading your own work on the computer, look for red and blue underlining. These lines mean that Word is giving you a suggestion for improvement. If you right click on the underlined word, the program suggests improvement.

Techniques

If no one is available and you are forced to be the one and only one to proofread your own work, you may want to use some special proofing techniques. These techniques would also be good for your proofreaders to follow.

Proofreading Techniques
Use a ruler to slow down your reading and make yourself read line by line.
Read the work out loud. This process slows down your reading and makes you listen to how it really sounds.
Read each line backward. The work will not make sense, but typographical errors will stand out more.
Limit your proofreading to small bits at any one time. You could take frequent breaks or limit yourself to a section or chapter a day. Try to do your final check the day after you finish writing.

Proofread when you are most fresh. This time may be early morning or whatever time of the day is your peak for best performance.
Try to proofread when you know you will have peace and quiet and can avoid interruptions from the telephone or visitors.
Be careful as on-screen proofreading is far more difficult than a printed copy.

Tips

Proofreading is a very important step—not to be neglected. Your computer may not catch all errors. During proofreading, you and your other proofreaders may find the following list helpful in looking for errors.

Proofreading Tips
Does the report make sense?
Are there any typographical errors?
Are words divided correctly throughout the document?
If right justification is used, should any words be force hyphenated to avoid large blank spaces between words?
Are words on the first and last lines of a page or paragraph divided?
Do you always have at least two lines in a paragraph on a page?
Do you have no more than 10-12 lines per paragraph?
Is the style consistent throughout—fonts, spacing, indenting, headings, etc.?
Is capitalization correct and consistent?
Is spelling correct and consistent?
Are numbers either given as figures or written out correctly and consistently?

Do quotation marks and parentheses always have both a beginning and an ending?
Do verbs and subjects agree?
Is the correct word used in words that sound alike—*their* and *there*; *two, to,* and *too*; *sense* and *cents, its* and *it's*, etc.?
Are complete sentences used, and do they make sense?
Are all numbers accurate?
Are all totals correctly added?

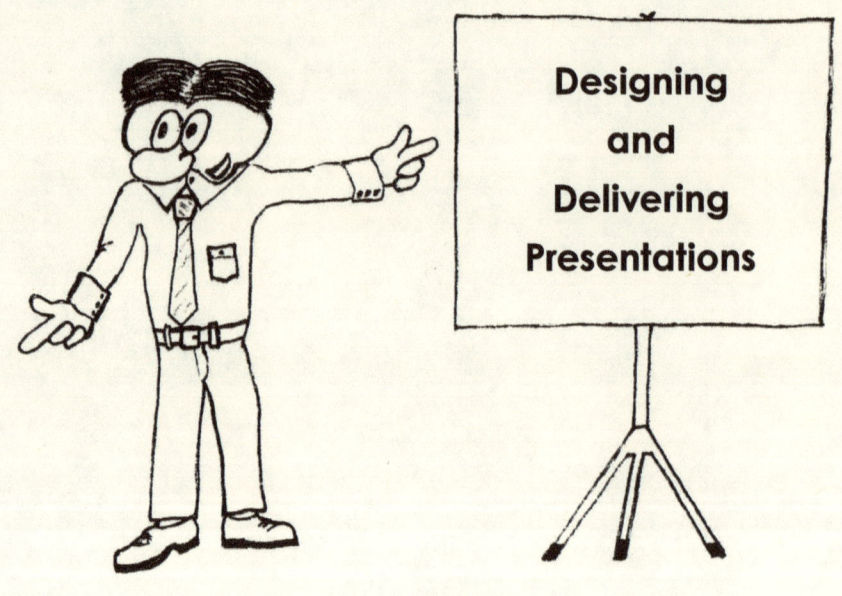

BONUS SECTION

Designing and Delivering Presentations

> *My co-author and I decided to add information on another kind of writing as a bonus section—designing and delivering presentations. Although similarities do exist, some differences are needed in preparing slides for a presentation. In general, the task represents short phases, lack of complete sentences, and no punctuation.*
>
> *I wrote the bonus section, but my co-author challenged me to think of the right- and left-brained people, who will be reading this book. Therefore, you have a choice to either read the printed words or look at the slides. For better understanding, you may want to both read and study the visuals. Slides are also a good solution in helping hearing-impaired people during a lecture.*
>
> *The challenge for me was that this book is to be printed without color and most clipart is illegal to use in a book. I hope it will help those of you liking visuals.*
>
> —Dr. Joyce Kupsh

Many times, writing needs to be presented orally to an audience. Orators, such as Winston Churchill, needed no visuals for supporting their presentation. However, most people can enhance their presentation by using visuals, such as slides shown using a computer and a projector. Many programs are available for making slides with the most popular one being Microsoft PowerPoint. Since it is packaged with Microsoft Office and has similar operating features to Word, Excel, and Publisher, users find it easy to learn and operate on a basic level.

Bonus Section

Designing & Delivering Presentations

Designing & Delivering Presentations

The Challenges

1. Designing the Slides
2. Delivering the Presentation

A first step in making a presentation is designing the slides. The real skill in making slides involves designing the slides for effective viewing. Slides should be designed to visually stimulate the audience. You don't need to be a graphic designer to design your slides but should be aware of a few basic principles. The second step is in using the slides during a presentation. Following a few basic procedures can lead to a more successful presentation with the result being an audience paying attention and absorbing your message.

The following sections list guidelines and tips for designing your slides as well as delivering the presentation using the slides. The authors prefer and use Microsoft PowerPoint, but many of the strategies can be applied to other software programs. Other software packages are available and can be found by searching for "slide packages for making presentations." However, the most frequently used software is Microsoft's PowerPoint.

Although many of the steps mentioned in the next section can apply to other programs, the following information is written for PowerPoint. This bonus section is not meant to be a "how to use software" but is a general view of tips and techniques in making effective presentations using PowerPoint. You may not be an orator, but you can be an effective presenter.

Tips for Designing Slides

Left-Brained People
- Logical Thinking
- Analysis
- Accuracy

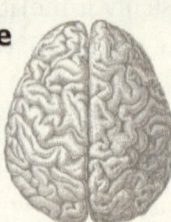

Right-Brained People
- Aesthetics
- Feeling
- Creativity

Tips for Designing Slides

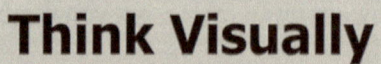
Think Visually

Designing Slides

You don't have a be a graphic artist to design interesting and creative slides for a presentation. The following general tips can help in making a presentation effective. Numerous studies have shown the value in making a presentation that will enhance and engage the audience. Scientists have determined that left-brain people focus on logical thinking, analysis, and accuracy, while right-brained subjects, on the other hand, focus on aesthetics, feeling, and creativity. Thus, the message is to think visually and develop slides accordingly. Other studies have shown that people remember 50 percent or more of what they see versus what they hear. Develop slides that are different from that of the written version.

Title Part
Body Part

- Make Slides Horizontal (Landscape) versus Vertical (Portrait)

- Use a Wide Screen Format—16 by 9 Versus 4 by 3

Template Choice

- Design Your Own

- Use Professionally Designed *(Available in Software)*

Template Choice

Slides should be made horizontally (landscape) versus vertically (portrait). With today's technology, a wide screen format should be chosen versus the standard format. Professionally designed templates are available with the software programs. Others can be purchased. A simple solution is to make your own template using the color palette using theme colors and variating the shades.

Two Parts—Title & Body

A slide should have two parts—the title and a body. The two should be separated by using a heavy line between the two parts, a box for the title, or a difference in color. This technique makes the viewer focus on what the slide is about and then the message of the slide.

Color

- Use Color Schemes of Your Company/Business
- Select Attractive Templates or Design Your Own
- Make Use of Graduated Colors—*2 or More Colors Blended*
- Consider Symbolism of Color Different in Other Countries/Cultures
- Remember Red on Green Not Good for Color-Impaired People

Color

Color is an effective communication tool. Even though this book is in black and white, a presentation can effectively use a variety of colors to enhance and visually stimulate an audience. Therefore, colors used in slides should be chosen carefully to carry out a theme of the message. In addition, color can capture attention, convey meanings, send a powerful message, relax or irritate the eyes, serve as a subliminally persuasive force, and in general create a more dynamic and energized design on slides.

Colors used do not have to be a solid color but can be graduated (blended together) for a more soothing look. A pure white background should be avoided since it can be a glare may be hard on the eyes. A light tint (such as gray, brown, or blue) prevents the glare. Slides can have a light background with dark letters or a dark background with light letters. The top part for the title can be one color with the message part another color.

The symbolism of color in different countries or cultures is a consideration in designing your slides. A web search for "color guide for different countries" can provide information for the meaning of colors in various countries.

Red on green or blue or the reverse should be avoided. Color-impaired people (referring to people with some degree of color blindness) may not be able to distinguish the words and see only gray.

WRITING: A SURVIVAL GUIDE

Font Choice

- **Make All Fonts Bold**
- **Select 2 Fonts—*1 for Heading & 1 for Body***

Example **Heading Arial Black Bold & Body Tahoma Bold**

Font Choice

Font selection is another consideration in designing slides. Bold type should be used to make the type more visible. Fonts are either serif (short cross strokes that project from the top or bottom of the main stroke of a letter) or sans serif (without any of the strokes).

A slide should use no more than two fonts—perhaps one for the heading and another for the body. The authors suggest a fat font for the title (such as Arial Black or Franklin Gothic Black) and a thinner font for the body (such as Tahoma or Arial). An advantage of Tahoma is that it gets more letters in a line, and yet, is easily read.

Using various font sizes makes for easier reading and better comprehension. Main points should be in a larger font size with secondary points a bit smaller.

Big Is Better

Font Sizes = **72 60 54 48** 36 24 20

- **Large Rooms Need Larger Sizes**
- **Nothing Under 20 Points for Screen Presentations**

Big Is Better

Yes, big is better. Fonts should be bold and large enough to be seen easily in the back of the room. The smallest size to be used is probably a 20-size font, but 24, 36, or more are much better. The larger the presentation room is the larger the fonts need to be.

Less Is Better

Rule of 49

- 7 Words on a Line on Text Lines
- 7 Text Lines on a Slide
- 49 Words Maximum on a Slide

In General Avoid

- Punctuation*
- Full Sentences

*Unless a Quotation or Purpose!

Less Is Better

Less is better on slides. Avoid filling the slide with words, which may mean that you are doing nothing but reading the words to your audience. A presenter should say more than what is on the slide. With bullet lists, the rule has evolved of 7 x 7 or Rule of 49—meaning no more than seven lines (down), and no more than seven words (across) on a line. However, even a total of 49 words (7 x 7) is overkill if used on every slide. The presenter ends up just reading the words on the slide, and the audience goes to sleep. A trend is to eliminate most if not all words using visual illustrations to represent the thought.

Parallel Construction

Verbs
- Inform . . .
- Relate . . .
- Make . . .
- Check . . .

or

Nouns
- Objects . . .
- Handouts . . .
- Audience . . .
- Questions . . .

*On an Individual Slide

Within each slide parallel construction should be used when making a bullet list. For instance, use all verbs such as *inform, relate, make,* and *check.* Or, if more appropriate for the slide, use all nouns such as *objects, handouts, audience,* and *questions.*

Graphics

Pictures   Illustrations   Clipart

Charts   Maps

Graphics
A Picture Is Worth Thousands of Words

Description of Soccer Ball

A soccer ball is an inflated round object shaped like a sphere with pentagon patches placed on other pentagon patches.

Graphics

The term graphics is used in referring to charts, illustrations, clipart, pictures, maps, or any visual representation. For instance, if using the words "stop sign" show a stop sign instead of the words. Thinking visually is a key technique in designing visuals. Many online graphics without a copyright (for students and business people), such as clipart and pictures, are available and can be found with a computer search. jpg and pdf files are smaller files than some of the other types of graphics; and therefore, they are appropriate for slides.

Music/Sounds/Videos

Music/Sounds/Videos

Music, sounds, or videos can enhance a slide package. Using music as an introduction before you start speaking can set the mood for the presentation. However, never try to speak when the music is playing. Sounds, such as a siren or a clock ticking, can be appropriately used. Voice clips of a quotation are also effective. YouTube has clips that may be appropriate for your presentation. Be sure that the clips are public domain. For insertion techniques, check the help menu or a manual for the software program being used. A search on YouTube can also be helpful in finding a clip with helpful procedures and directions for making the insertion.

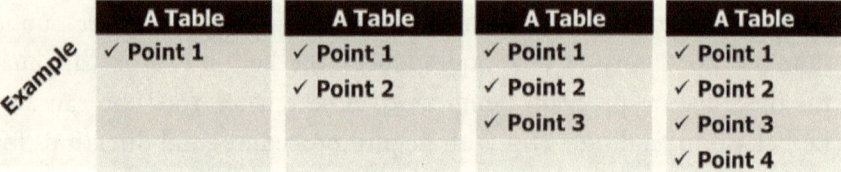

Animations

Animation techniques create movement within a slide. For instance, you can build on points and other inserts on the slide as you speak. This technique helps the audience to focus on what is being said versus trying to absorb the whole slide and not really listening to your voice. Building a chart with animation is also helpful as well as creating interest with appropriate clipart to illustrate your message. Remember the technique of "less is better" and build your slide as you speak.

Transitions

Movement Between Slides

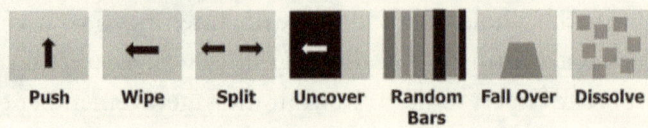

Examples: Push, Wipe, Split, Uncover, Random Bars, Fall Over, Dissolve

Plus Many Other Ways to Move from Slide to Slide

Transitions

Transitions refer to the movement between slides. Choices can be dissolve, checkerboard, swivel, boxed in, or boxed out plus many more depending upon the software program being used. One method should be chosen to prevent the viewers of wondering how the next slide going to come in on the screen. Exceptions can be made if wanting to change to a new topic or subject.

Speaker Notes

- ➢ **Inserted Below Slide for Speaker Only**
- ➢ **Should Not Be Read but for Reminders**
- ➢ **Can Be Setup at Podium Showing**
    - Present Slide
    - Speaker Notes
    - Next Slide

Speaker Notes

Many of the software programs allow speaker notes to be inserted below the actual slide. Such notes are valuable to use when practicing or rehearsing the presentation to remind a speaker of the important points and issues you wanted to include. Numbers and statistics that might be hard to remember can be helpful when placed in the speaker notes. However, a speaker should not read directly from the speaker notes; thus, the notes should be brief. PowerPoint allows a setup where the computer at the speaker's podium shows the slide, the notes, and the next slide to be shown; but the audience sees only the slide.

Delivering Presentations

Speaking is frequently a scary problem for many people. After designing appropriate, creative, and stimulating slides, you are still the main feature. The slides can support and lead you through the presentation. Before the presentation, preparation steps can be taken to make it more comfortable. However, remember that one should never be too comfortable, or it may mean the lack of caring. Professional football, basketball, and soccer players are always nervous before a big game, but they take steps in their preparation to avoid any projected crises that may occur.

Delivering a Presentation with Slides

Practice / Rehearse

Do Not Memorize
Word for Word

Timing

A Timing Device
Can Be Set to Record
Amount of Time
on Each Slide & Total Time

Practice/Rehearse/Timing

The first step in preparation is practice, practice, practice/rehearsal/rehearsal/rehearsal. A presentation should not be written and memorized word for word. Instead, the slides and points or illustrations within should trigger what is to be said. Many times, a presenter is given a specific timeframe. PowerPoint provides a feature to time a presentation during rehearsals showing how much time is spent on each slide.

If slides are prepared well in advance of the presentation date, a person can rehearse many times. Changes to the slides may become apparent, and the timing can be perfected.

Equipment Setup

- Check Out Equipment Before the Presentation
- Make Slides Fill the Screen
- Check Slides from Back of Room for Size of Fonts
- Use Remote Control with Laser Pointer

Equipment Setup

Equipment should be tested in advance of the presentation to be sure everything works properly. A mistake sometimes made is that the slides do not completely fill the projection screen. After setting up the slides, go to the very back of the room and see how the slides look. Can they be viewed easily? If not, make the font size larger. Proofreading from a distance can tend to show up any errors or how the slides can be made better. Test to be sure that any insertions such as sounds or videos work properly. If you are using another computer, you may find that things look differently or do not work properly.

A remote control with a laser pointer gives a speaker the ability to focus the audience on a specific point or illustration. The remote is used to move to the next slide and still be away from the computer. Most remotes are not connected to the computer and allow presenters to move about the room. They do not need to be pointed at the projection screen or the computer.

Speaker Position

Stand to the Audience's Left of Screen

Speaker Position

As a rule, a speaker should stand on the audience's left side of the screen. The reason is that the speaker should be the focus with the slides a secondary backup. People in most countries read from left to right so the eyes of the audience should be on the speaker and then move on to the slides.

A podium is helpful for speaker use if a person is not so short that he/she is barely seen. A laptop on the podium can be setup (with PowerPoint) so that the speaker sees the present slide, the next slide, and a few speaker notes.

Speaking Essentials

- **Body Movement**—Stand Stationary/Can Do Slow Walk
- **Voice Projection**—Use Microphone if Necessary to Be Heard
- **Ice Breakers/Humor**—Can Help if Appropriate
- **Body Language & Gestures**—Make Them Natural to Emphasize
- **Transitions**—Change of Voice, Pause, and/or Black Screen

Speaking Essentials

Speaking essentials can involve a whole course or book. The following are some key points for a speaker to remember when presenting with slides.

Body Movement. The body can remain stationary behind the podium, but a slow walk or movement can be effective in reaching out to engage the audience. However, a presenter should be careful not block the screen. In general, a fast walk or a waltzing movement of the feet can be distracting and show nervousness.

Voice Projection. Projecting the voice is necessary so that you can be heard throughout the room. Be sure that your voice continues to be loud enough to be heard throughout the room. A microphone may be necessary to accomplish this task.

Body Language and Gestures. Body language and gestures are important in conveying a message. Gestures should be natural to emphasize a point being made, but the larger the room the larger the gestures need to be. Eye contact with members of the audience is essential versus looking down at the podium. Pick out friendly faces from the back of the room, each side of the room, and in front and focus on these friendly faces to boost your confidence. Eye contact makes the listeners think you are speaking directly to them.

Transitions. Moving from one topic/subject to another should be made obvious and smoothly. A change of voice can also show a transition. Some remotes can project a black screen in case a presenter wants to discuss some topic and does not have a slide on the screen. If not, a complete black slide can be inserted in making the slides. A slide is distracting if it is not the subject of the discussion.

Speaking Essentials

- **Real Objects**—Can Be Helpful if Large Enough
- **Handouts**—Use Before/During/After?
- **Audience Interaction**—Engage the Audience
- **Questions & Answers**—Save for Last if Timing Is Necessary

Real objects. In addition to the slides, real objects can be helpful in a presentation if they are large enough to be seen throughout the room. Smaller objects can be passed around. Displays can also be used for the audience to view before/during/after the presentation.

Handouts. Copies of the slides can be printed (in PowerPoint) in regular size; but to save paper, they can also be made as handouts with 2, 3, 4, 6, or 9 on a page for the audience. Handouts are sometimes valuable but can also be distracting. A presenter may not want the audience to see what is coming next. In addition, the question should be asked as to whether the slides as a handout are valuable for the audience to have. Perhaps just a few of the slides should be printed, or there may be other materials that the audience might find valuable as a handout. If a presenter finds the handouts left in the room or in a waste basket, the message is clear that the audience did not find anything on the slides that they wanted to take with them. A message for the next time!

Audience Interaction. Interacting with the audience is helpful in being sure that they are engaged. Questions requiring short answers or a show of hands as well as allowing for a stand-up-stretch break are ways of keeping an audience engaged. People like to participate, but you are the presenter and may have a timeframe for presenting so be careful to keep interaction and engagements in control. If no timeframe, audience interaction is a way of seeing if the audience is listening and really with you. Icebreakers that tie into the presentation can make an audience feel comfortable. However, never tell a joke just to tell a joke. People like and enjoy humor if appropriately used. Avoid politics, race, sex, and any other inappropriate topics. In a large room, a microphone may be necessary.

Questions and answers. You may be save questions for the end of the presentations in order to remain on a time schedule. If this practice is to be followed, the audience should be asked at the beginning of the presentation to jot down the questions on a card that is passed out and asked to hold their questions until the end of the presentation. Other times, a presenter may prefer to take the questions as they occur if more appropriate and time allows.

Checklists

Use the checklists as a tool in the following instances:

- Before you write
- While you are writing
- After the first draft
- When you are finished

For each question, answer one of the following:

_____ Yes
_____ No

If your answer is No or you are not sure, review the appropriate section and confirm that your project is correct, or change the incorrect parts. If your answer is No or you are not sure, check the contents or the index for the page number to find the information regarding that topic.

Chapter 1

Purpose	Yes	No
Have you determined the purpose of your writing? Inform Interpret Recommend Persuade		

Type	Yes	No
Have you determined the type project you are going to write?		
Research Report		
Case Study Analysis		
Case Study		
Feasibility Study		
Strategic Plan		
Business Plan		
Business Proposal		
Evaluation Report		
Synthesis Report		
Assessment/Audit Report		
Technical Report		
Follow-up Report		
Press Release		
Miscellaneous		

Format Style	Yes	No
Have you determined what format style is appropriate?		
Essay		
E-mail, Memo, Letter		
Form		
Report		
Newsletter		
Brochure		
Magazine, Booklet, or Manual		
Social Media		

Report Parts	Yes	No
Do you have all the necessary parts?		
Executive Summary/Abstract		
Title Page		
Contents		
Introduction		
Body		
Bibliography/References/Resources		
Appendices		

Chapter 2

Planning	Yes	No
Did you have a detailed scheme or method worked out beforehand for the accomplishment of an objective?		
Did you establish an organized overall plan?		
Are the purposes and objectives of your writing clearly stated?		
Did you set up a time schedule for each of the sections?		
Is your project written for the target audienc: • What is the educational level of the intended audience? • How much background or technical experience do members of your intended audience have on the topic? • Will the audience be expecting a formal or informal report? • What type of action—a verbal response, a written reaction, or an interview—anticipate from the audience? • Are you addressing the appropriate audience?		

Researching	Yes	No
Did you collect the data?		
Did you include enough relevant existing sources?		
Did you include the relevant original sources?		
Do you have a complete, organized list of what is to be covered?		
Do you have a parallel hierarchy of topics and subtopics?		
Are the topics and subtopics descriptive and functional rather than attention-getting ones?		
Are there two or more points within each subtopic?		
Do you have a logical sequential arrangement of topics and subtopics?		

Outlining	Yes	No
Do you have a complete, organized list of what is to be covered in the project?		
Do you have a parallel hierarchy of topics and subtopics?		
Are the topics and subtopics descriptive and functional rather than attention-getting ones?		
Are there two or more points within each subtopic?		
Do you have a logical or sequential arrangement of topics and subtopics?		

Chapter 3

Avoiding Plagiarism	Yes	No
Did you avoid all the forms of plagiarism listed by The Writing Studio at Colorado State?		
Did you follow the guidelines for avoiding plagiarism?		
Did you cite the reference when you paraphrased or summarized words of ideas?		
Did you use quotation marks and cite the reference where you used the exact words of someone?		
Did you reference or give credit if you used a paper from a previous class?		

Technology-Based Tools	Yes	No
Did you follow the advice for using technology-based tools?		
Did you make use of reference management software, citation creators, and/or word processing software?		

Outlining	Yes	No
Do you have a complete, organized list of what is to be covered in the project?		
Do you have a parallel hierarchy of topics and subtopics?		
Are the topics and subtopics descriptive and functional rather than attention-getting ones?		
Are there two or more points within each subtopic?		
Do you have a logical or sequential arrangement of topics and subtopics?		

CHECKLISTS

Citing Sources	Yes	No
Did you block or indent direct quotations of 5 lines or more than 40 words by indenting from both margins by approximately 5 spaces or half an inch?		
Did you insert your comments between brackets in the quotations?		
Did you indicate omissions from the original quote by using ellipsis points—a series of three periods (. . .)?		
Did you include a quotation of less than 5 lines or 40 words in the text using quotation marks to distinguish it from your writing?		
Did you select only the most relevant portion if a direct quotation is more than a page or so in length or simply refer to it in the text of the report and include it as an appendix?		
Did you mention in the report at the appropriate place items in the appendix?		
Did you paraphrase or summarize (restating material in your own words) as an indirect quotation?		
Even though quotation marks are not used, could a reader tell exactly what is paraphrased and what is your own work by using the following: to Xxx, . . . ; Xxx states that . . .; Xxx found that . . . ?		
Did you use either (1) parenthetical references, (2) footnotes, or () endnotes?		
In parenthetical references, did you place a shortened reference within the text?		
Did you include a complete listing of these sources at the end of the section, chapter, or report?		

Did you place the last name of the author and the date in parentheses separated by a comma for parenthetical references? The name of a corporation, the name of a work, or some other means of identification may also be used with the date.		
If the author's name is mentioned in the text, did you use only the date in parentheses? If you refer to both the author and the date in the text, nothing needs to be put in parentheses.		
Did you include the reference in the alphabetical listing at the end?		
If the quote is from a specific page, did you include the page number in case a reader wants to locate the original writing?		
Did you indicate endnotes in the text by a raised number, or a number in parenthesis on the same line as the text?		
Did you delete any footnotes at the bottom of the page if you used endnotes?		
Did you include a complete listing of the sources in numerical order at the end of the report along with an alphabetized list of those same references?		
Did you use footnotes correctly by placing a raised number in the text at the end of the quotation—either direct or paraphrased and then placing the identification at the bottom of the page under a one-inch line?		
Did you use a complete listing of the reference the first time it appears?		
Did you use a shortened version of the subsequent references to the same work?		

Chapter 4

Objectivity	Yes	No
Did you write your project from an objective standpoint?		
Did you eliminate any personal emotions and opinions?		
Does your work include facts and findings?		
Do your facts and findings lead to recommendations and conclusions formed on the basis of those facts and findings?		
Did you look at all sides of the problem with an open mind before stating your conclusions?		
Did you take on the role of a referee at a sporting event or a judge presiding in course?		
Are your decisions based on the results, the evidence, or an interpretation of the results and evidence?		
Did you use proper nouns and the occasional use of *he, him, she, her, they,* and *them?*		

Conciseness	Yes	No
Did you eliminate information that is irrelevant to the report?		
Did you eliminate redundancy—useless repetition of words?		
Did you combine clutter and clichés in a way that does not waste words?		
Did you use compound adjectives to reduce the number of words?		
Did you substitute a precise word or words for phrases?		
Did you avoid restating implied (obvious) ideas?		
Did you cite specific examples for each abstract word?		

Coherence	Yes	No
Is your writing coherent by linking the thought from one sentence to the next and from one paragraph to the next?		
Did you link by repeating words and by using a transition?		
Did you repeat a word either directly or with a similar word?		
Did you use transitional words—such as an explanation, enumeration or listing, similarity or contrast, and cause or effect, as well as to, for examples, for instance, to illustrate.		
Did you use bullet lists with numbers or symbols when appropriate?		
Did you use transition words to show a similarity or a contrast between two situations?		
Did you use transitional words—such as because of, therefore, thus, as a result, for this reason, consequently—to show a cause or an effect?		

Tone	Yes	No
Did you accentuate the positive and eliminate the negative?		
Did you write in active voice—with the subject doing the acting?		
Did you avoid expletives—*such as there are, it is, it is noted that, it is understood that, etc.*?		
Did you use a noun or the pronouns *he, she, him, her, they*, and *them (avoiding* I, my, we, our*)*?		

	Yes	No
Did you eliminate any tone in your writing that reflects a gender bias or any other type of bias—*race, religion, age, disability, or ethnic group?*		
Did you avoid stereotyping by changing to plural form when possible or referring to both genders?		
Did you eliminate the use of biased titles and substitute a more neutral word?		
Emphasis	**Yes**	**No**
Did you decide on your most important word or phrase and then decide whether you want that word or phrase to make an initial or a lasting impact?		
Variety & Comprehensive	**Yes**	**No**
Did you vary the length of sentences and paragraphs and mix simple sentences with complex or compound sentences?		
Does your report include all the necessary parts?		

Chapter 5

Abbreviations	Yes	No
Did you use abbreviations correctly and appropriately?		

Acronyms	Yes	No
Did you use acronyms that your audience knows?		
Did you spell out the acronym the first time it was used?		
Did you include a list of acronyms after the table of contents?		

Capitalization	Yes	No
Did you capitalize the: • first word of a sentence, • first word of a direct quotation, • first word following a colon, • names of specific things?		

Italics	Yes	No
Did you use italics to: • indicate names of books, magazines, newspapers, plays, and movies, • mix foreign words with English words, • place emphasis or highlight a word, • refer to a word as a word?		

Numbers	Yes	No
Did you use the following rules for numbers: • Spell out numbers for one through ten. • Use figures for numbers larger than ten. • Spell out numbers if the first word of a sentence. • Use figures in a listing when one of the numbers is higher than ten. • Use figures to express dates without *th* unless the number is before the month. • Use figures to express sums of money. • Use figures to express chapter and page numbers. • Use figures to express decimals, percentage, dimensions, weights, and temperatures. • Omit the zeroes and decimals unless other numbers in the same sentence include cents. • Use words to represent time when *o'clock* is used but figures with *p.m.* or *a.m.* • Omit the minutes unless another time is used in the same sentence where they are needed. • Use words for names of streets up to and including twelve?		

Punctuation	Yes	No
Did you use punctuation (apostrophe, colon, comma, dash, diagonal, ellipsis points, exclamation, hyphen, parentheses, period, question mark, quotation marks, semicolon, and underscore) correctly?		

Spelling	Yes	No
Did you use the spellcheck?		
Did you evaluate your report for errors that may not be found by the spellcheck?		
Did you have someone else check for errors?		

Word Division	Yes	No
Did you avoid the division of words: • in the first and last lines of a paragraph or page, • in more than two lines in a row, • if only one letter is left on the first line, • if only five or fewer letters?		
Did you divide: • only between syllables, • compound words between the two words, • words containing a hyphen at the hyphen?		
Did you keep a single-vowel syllable with the first part of the word?		

Chapter 6

Fonts	Yes	No
Did you choose an appropriate font(s) from the four classifications for your work?		
Did you take advantage or use any of the variations below? • plain, bold, italics, • condensed, narrow, expanded, • thickness, • uppercase, lowercase, • underscoring, • reverse type, • drop caps		
Did you avoid underlining except for websites and e-mail addresses?		
Is the font for the body of your project between 8 and 12 points?		
Did you use appropriate line spacing?		
Did you make appropriate use of right/center/left alignment?		
If you justified the margins, did you avoid large blank spaces?		

Color	Yes	No
Did you take advantage of color (if appropriate) as follows: • quick identification of sections. • glossaries or appendices to allow for easy referencing. • section or chapter heading of each new section. • colored covers and a neutral white, off-white, or beige for the inside. • fonts as long as they are easy to read?		

Paper	Yes	No
Did you select an appropriate weight of paper?		

Layout	Yes	No
Did you determine whether a landscape or portrait layout was more appropriate?		
Were margins reasonable?		
Did you leave room for the binding?		
Is the column size reasonable?		
Is there sufficient blank space on each page?		
Did you make headings and subheadings concise but descriptive?		
Do you have parallel construction using all verbs or all nouns?		
Did you break the divisions down so that a heading or subheading always has two or more listings?		

Did you make the headings and subheadings agree with the table of contents?		
Are your pages numbered correctly?		
Did you make use of headers and footers?		
Is your work attractively bound?		
Did you use an attractive cover?		

Graphics	Yes	No
Does your project include graphics as needed to help the readers?		
Did you include lines, boxes, shapes, background tints, and patterns?		
Did you include clip art and photos as appropriate?		
Did you use tables to list items in addition to bullet lists?		
When using numbers, did you display them as charts or graphs?		

Chapter 7

Edit	Yes	No
Is the material complete?		
Should any of the content be omitted?		
Is the information correct?		
Is the content presented in the right order?		
Is any reorganization needed?		
Are there better ways of presenting some of the information, such as graphs, tables, artwork, etc.?		
Does any rewriting need to be done?		
Did you follow the style from one of the style manuals?		
Did you follow the style or rules for your particular company or a style requested by your teacher?		
Are you consistent in details of your style?		

Proofread	Yes	No
Have you read using a ruler to slow down your reading and make yourself read line by line?		
Did you read the writing out loud?		
Did you read each line backward?		
Did you limit your proofreading to small bits at any one time?		
Did you proofread when you are most fresh?		
Did you try to proofread when you know you will have peace and quiet and can avoid interruptions from the telephone or visitors?		
Does the report make sense?		
Are there any typographical errors?		

Are words divided correctly throughout the document?		
If right justification is used, should any words be force hyphenated to avoid large blank spaces between words?		
Did you avoid having words on the first and last lines of a page or paragraph divided?		
Do you always have at least two lines in a paragraph on a page?		
Is the style consistent throughout—fonts, spacing, indenting, headings, etc.?		
Is capitalization correct and consistent?		
Is spelling correct and consistent?		
Are numbers either given as figures or written out correctly and consistently?		
Do quotation marks and parentheses always have both a beginning and an ending?		
Do verbs and subjects agree?		
Is the correct word used in words that sound alike—*their* and *there*; *two*, *to*, and *too*; *sense* and *cents*, *its* and *it's*, etc.?		
Are complete sentences used and do they make sense?		
Are all numbers accurate?		
Are all totals correctly added?		

Bonus Section

Designing Presentations	Yes	No
Are you considering both left- and right-brained people in the audience?		
Is your presentation visually stimulating?		
Do you have an appropriate template?		
Did you use a wide-screen format?		
Do you have a clear division of the heading from the body?		
Does your color scheme make an attractive design?		
Is your font choice clear and large enough for the size of your presentation room?		
Did you follow the Rule of 49?		
Are your graphics and illustrations appropriate and helpful?		
Did you use analytics and graphics?		
Did you include any appropriate music, sounds, or video clips that would added to the presentation?		
Did you use animations to help the audience focus on particular points you are addressing?		
Did you use a transition to move between slides?		
Did you include any (short) speaker notes?		
Have you practiced/rehearsed using a timer?		
Did you use the timing device to get a time for each slide?		

Delivering Presentations	Yes	No
Did you check your equipment setup and try the slides to be sure everything is working correctly?		
Are you going to be standing to the audience's left of the screen?		
Have you decided whether appropriate to stand stationary or do a slow walk?		
Are you able to project your voice to be heard throughout the room or should you have a microphone?		
Do you need an ice breaker?		
Have you considered how some appropriate humor can be included?		
Have you considered your body language and appropriate gestures?		
Are you making proper transitions between topics?		
Is it appropriate to include/have any real objects to show?		
If you are using handouts, have you decided the appropriate distribution time?		
Do you have ways of engaging the audience?		
Have you decided whether to ask the audience to answer questions as they arise or save questions until the end of your presentation?		

Index

A

abbreviations
abstract
abstract or general words
acronyms
active vs passive
alignment
animations
APA reference list
Apostrophe
appendices
appendix
assessment report
audit report
avoiding plagiarism

B

bias-free language
bibliographies
binding
blank space
blogs
body
booklet
brochure
business plan
business proposal

C

capitalization
case study
case study analysis
charts and graphs
checklists
citation creators
citing sources
    endnotes
    footnotes
    parenthetical
clutter and clichés
coherence
colon
color
    color-impaired
    graduated
    on slides
column size
comma
comprehensive
conciseness
consistency
contents
cover
cover letter

D

dash
data, types of
   primary
   secondary
delivering presentations
designing slides
diagonal
drop cap

E

editing
   consistency
   style
   substance
ellipsis
e-mail
emphasis
endnotes
essay
evaluation report
exclamation point
executive summary/abstract
expletives
extra phrases

F

feasibility study
follow-up report
font alignment
fonts
   papers
   size
   slides
format styles

G

graphics
   chart (graph)
   icons (symbols)
   logos
   photographs

H

halftone
handouts
headers and footers
headings and subheadings
hyphen

I

implied ideas
inform
interpret
introduction
irrelevant information
italics

L

layout
leaders
line spacing

M

magazine
margins

N

Newsletter
Numbers

INDEX

O

objectives
objectivity
organization
outline
overall plan

P

page numbers
page orientation
paper
paraphrasing
parenthetical
parentheses
period
persuade
plagiarism
positive vs. negative
press release
primary data
pronouns
proofreading
punctuation
punctuation marks
    apostrophe
    colon
    comma
    dash
    diagonal
    ellipsis points
    exclamation points
    hyphen
    parentheses
    period
    question mark
    quotation marks
    semicolon
    underscore

purposes of written projects
    inform
    interpret
    persuade
    recommend

Q

question mark
quotation marks

R

recommend
redundancy
reference checkers
reference management software
repetition
reports, parts of
    appendix
    bibliography
    body
    contents
    executive summary
    introduction
    title page
research reports, types
    assessment
    business plan
    business proposal
    case study
    case study analysis
    evaluation
    feasibility study
    follow-up
    press release
    research
    synthesis
    technical

researching
resume

S

secondary data
semicolon
social media
sources
    primary
    secondary
speaker
    audience interaction
    body language
    essentials
    notes
    position
spelling
stereotyping
strategic plan
style
substance
summaries
synthesis report

T

target audience
technical report
text size
time schedule
tone
transition
    slides
    words

U

using style manuals

V

Variety

W

word division
writing style
writing style techniques
    coherence
    comprehensiveness
    conciseness
    emphasis
    objectivity
    tone
    variety

www.ingramcontent.com/pod-product-compliance
Lightning Source LLC
LaVergne TN
LVHW041813060526
838201LV00046B/1243